JEFFERSON COUNTY LIBRARY
620 Cedar Avenue
Port Hadlock, WA 98339
(360) 385-6544   www.jclibrary.info

DATE DUE

DEC 1 4	

DEMCO, INC. 38-2971

Y0-CAW-564

Sitting Bull

Legends of the Wild West

Sitting Bull

Billy the Kid

Calamity Jane

Buffalo Bill Cody

Crazy Horse

Davy Crockett

Wyatt Earp

Geronimo

Wild Bill Hickok

Jesse James

Nat Love

Annie Oakley

Legends of the Wild West

Sitting Bull

Ronald A. Reis

CHELSEA HOUSE
PUBLISHERS
An imprint of Infobase Publishing

Chelsea House
An imprint of Infobase Publishing
132 West 31st Street
New York NY 10001

Library of Congress Cataloging-in-Publication Data
Reis, Ronald A.
  Sitting Bull / Ronald A. Reis.
      p. cm. — (Legends of the Wild West)
  Includes bibliographical references and index.
  ISBN 978-1-60413-527-5 (hardcover)
  1. Sitting Bull, 1831-1890—Juvenile literature. 2. Dakota Indians—Biography—Juvenile literature. 3. Hunkpapa Indians—Biography—Juvenile literature. 4. Little Bighorn, Battle of the, Mont., 1876—Juvenile literature. I. Title. II. Series.
  E99.D1R35 2010
  978.004'9752—dc22
  [B]   2009041339

Chelsea House books are available at special discounts when purchased in bulk quantities for businesses, associations, institutions, or sales promotions. Please call our Special Sales Department in New York at (212) 967-8800 or (800) 322-8755.

You can find Chelsea House on the World Wide Web at
http://www.chelseahouse.com

Text design by Kerry Casey
Cover design by Keith Trego
Composition by EJB Publishing Services
Cover printed by Bang Printing, Brainerd, Minn.
Book printed and bound by Bang Printing, Brainerd, Minn.
Date printed: March, 2010
Printed in the United States of America

10 9 8 7 6 5 4 3 2 1

This book is printed on acid-free paper.

All links and Web addresses were checked and verified to be correct at the time of publication. Because of the dynamic nature of the Web, some addresses and links may have changed since publication and may no longer be valid.

CONTENTS

1 Muffled Cries   7

2 The Lakota Way   16

3 Wasichu Challenge   26

4 Determined Foe   36

5 Hostiles and Friendlies   46

6 Soldiers Upside Down   58

7 Winter of Discontent   69

8 Grandmother's Refuge   78

9 Celebrity Prisoner   88

10 Hunkpapa Patriot   98

Chronology and Timeline   108

Glossary   112

Bibliography   115

Further Resources   119

Picture Credits   121

Index   122

About the Author   126

MUFFLED CRIES

Just 14 years old in 1845, "Slow," as the Hunkpapa youth was called, sought to prove himself in battle. Like all young men of his Plains Indian tribe, he wanted to enter the coveted warrior ranks.

His nickname in no way implied dim-wittedness, but rather a thoughtful hesitancy before plunging into new endeavors. Yet on this scorching midsummer day, Slow, as he raced his powerful gray mount to meet up with 10 Hunkpapa tribal warriors off to gather scalps, horses, and glory, decided to take a risk. He would beg his older warrior "brothers," one of whom was his father, to take him along, to allow him, young and generally untested as he was, to duel against the hated Crow. In doing so, Slow hoped to gain his moment in the sun, to garner his first coup (pronounced "coo"), or victory against an enemy.

With Slow reluctantly accepted, the war party proceeded up the Powder River (in what is now central and north-central Wyoming) to search for adversaries. On the third day out, a dozen mounted Crow were spotted beside a creek. As the Hunkpapa immediately charged, the Crow spread out, with one warrior attempting to escape. Slow, his naked body (except for a breechcloth) painted yellow from head to foot, shrieked a war cry and galloped in pursuit. Pulling abreast of the Crow (who had notched an arrow, ready to shoot), Slow smashed his foe with a tomahawk, knocking him from his mount. A fellow Hunkpapa quickly finished the fallen warrior.

Slow, however, by making contact with an enemy, had counted this as his first coup. In an instant, he had become a Hunkpapa warrior.

That evening, Slow's proud father gave a feast, during which he boasted about his son's exploits. Slow was presented with a white feather, to be placed upright in the hair as a symbol of his first coup. The father substituted a fine bay horse for the boy's gray. And the older Hunkpapa painted his son black all over in a token of victory before leading him around the camp to great applause.

In the ultimate accolade, however, the father awarded Slow the elder's name. Born Jumping Badger but nicknamed Slow, from now on the youthful warrior, with ability so aptly demonstrated this day, would be known as *Tatanka-Iyotanka*, or Sitting Bull. The name, according to Robert Utley, author of *The Lance and the Shield,* "suggested an animal possessed of great endurance, his build much admired by the people, and when brought to bay planted immovably on his haunches to fight on to the death." Such would reflect Sitting Bull's life, his story, to the day the proud Hunkpapa died.

SILENCE IS GOLDEN

Within minutes, perhaps seconds, of his birth in 1831, Sitting Bull was, according to custom, forced into silence, his baby cries muffled, or snuffed out. The boy's mother, Her-Holy-Door, immediately took her infant son's nose, as he puckered to release a scream, between her thumb and forefinger, with her palm placed gently over his mouth. The boy's cry thus suppressed, he twisted for breath and his mother let go, but only a little. At the first sign of another cry, his air would be cut off again.

And so it would go, with Sitting Bull's mother day after day, weaning her newborn into silence. According to Mari Sandoz, author of *These Were the Sioux*:

> During the newborn minutes, that newborn hour, Indian children, boy and girl, were taught the first and greatest lesson of their lives: that no one could be permitted

Sitting Bull, one of the most important figures in American Indian history, was a member of the Hunkpapa tribe of the Plains region. Raised to be tough and fearless, he became a warrior at an early age and later, as an adult, the leader of a union of tribes and nations militantly opposed to the westward expansion of the U.S. government.

to endanger the people by even one cry to guide a roving
enemy to the village or to spoil a hunt that could mean
the loss of the winter meat for a whole band or even a
small tribe.

In the years to come, as a Hunkpapa boy would be taken out at
night to guard the village or horse herd, he would be expected to
endure the greatest of pains with only a small whimper. If he fell
from the limb of a high tree, he would fight, clenching his teeth, to
remain silent. Thus a young American Indian prepared himself to
be the silent stalker of human enemies and grazing buffalo.

That rival warrior bands prowled the Plains looking for a fight,
there was no doubt. True, in many cases, the ensuing battles were
scarcely more dangerous than hard-fought football games of today.
But in struggles for hunting grounds, or when warriors went out on
revenge raids, the situation could quickly get ugly. Utley spared no
feelings when he declared, "Men, women, and children of all ages
expected to be killed if seized or cornered, their scalps and other
parts of the body torn off as trophies, their remains hacked and dis-
figured as a permanent affliction in the spirit world."

Silence, at the right moment, was not only golden, but
lifesaving.

NOMADS OF THE PLAINS

Sitting Bull was born a Sioux. For an American Indian in the fourth
decade of the nineteenth century, that was considered a good thing.
The Sioux Nation reigned as a superpower throughout the Northern Plains. The total Sioux homeland took in a vast area centered
in what is now South Dakota, but it also spread west into Montana
and Wyoming, north into North Dakota, east into Minnesota, and
south into Nebraska. Smaller tribes in the region feared the mighty
Sioux and paid them tribute.

The nation itself was (and still is) divided into three distinct
groups. In the east, in the Minnesota woodlands, were the Dakota.
Farther west, into America's prairie region, the Nakota lived. And

out west, on the vast Plains, were the Lakota. The Lakota probably numbered no more than 20,000 to 30,000 in 1830.

The Lakota culture was (according to Utley) hardly a generation old at the time of Sitting Bull's birth. It was only at the beginning of the nineteenth century that they fully transitioned from pedestrians to mounted nomads. On horseback, the Lakota ranged, east to west, from the high Plains between the Missouri River and the Bighorn Mountains, to the Canadian prairies to the north and the Platte and Republican rivers to the south.

Within the Lakota grouping were seven tribes, one of which was the Hunkpapa ("gatekeepers"). It was into this large grouping, with its approximately 500 lodges, sheltering 3,500 individuals, that Sitting Bull was brought silently into the world.

The ability of any Plains Indian tribe, particularly the Hunkpapas, to travel far and wide rested entirely on the back, literally, of the amazing horse. Brought north out of Mexico by the Spanish centuries earlier, the horse first penetrated the southern and then the northern Plains. Tribes everywhere begged, borrowed, stole, or traded with one another for what the Sioux soon came to call *sunka wakan*, the "sacred dog." It was a just tribute. After all, compared to the dog, the horse ranged farther, pulled larger and heavier loads, and most remarkably, bore a rider. To the Hunkpapa, the horse was, indeed, *wakan*—powerful and sacred.

The horse enabled the Plains Indians to break out into a full-time nomadic life. As Thomas Mails declared in *The Mystic Warriors of the Plains*:

> Before this they [the Plains Indians] were semi-nomadic, with small bands of Indian families moving out at intervals from fairly stationary villages to hunt buffalo at piskins and buffalo jumps. With the horse to carry them, their tipis [also spelled "tepees"], and their other possessions, they could follow the roving buffalo herds throughout the good-weather months, and they could raid the enemy's horse herds at greater distances in shorter periods of time.

It was this ability, above all, to hunt buffalo in a new and more effective way that elevated the horse to its exalted status and allowed Plains Indians, most notably the Hunkpapa-Lakota, to enter into their mid-nineteenth-century golden age.

BUFFALO RUNNERS

Just how many buffalo (also known as bison) roamed the vast Great Plains at the time of Sitting Bull no one knows. Dale Lott, a noted authority on the subject, put the number at 30 million, though less-informed investigators are often willing to double that figure. No matter, 30 million is an awesome number. Early travelers could spend days moving cautiously among the plodding mammals. Some herds stretched for mile upon mile, covering the land from one horizon to the next.

It was a good thing there were so many buffalo, for by the early 1800s Plains Indians had become totally dependent on every inch of the animal for their wants and for their survival. According to the authors of *Indian Wars*:

> Buffalo meat was the principal Indian food. From the hide came robes for warmth and trade and skins for the distinctive conical tepee that sheltered the family. Hides, stomach, and intestines were fashioned into containers for cooking, storage, and transport, bones into tools. Even the dried droppings, buffalo chips, made fuel when wood was scarce.

To bring a buffalo down, to slay it for all these uses, was not an easy task, however. Only the most able tribal hunters were up to the challenge.

Key to accomplishing the deed was, of course, the horse. Not any horse would do, to be sure, but only one groomed specifically for the task, one with breakaway speed that could also stop short and make quick turns. Known as a "buffalo runner," the animal would be drilled from an early age to race and parallel any galloping

Buffalo was a major resource for many Native American tribes and nations. One animal could provide meat for food, skins for clothes and teepees, bones for tools and weapons, and more. At an early age, Sitting Bull knew how important the buffalo were to his people and killed his first buffalo calf when he was 10 years old.

bison, a beast the horse instinctively knew was more powerful and faster than it.

Since a rider required the use of both hands to work his favorite killing weapon, the all but silent bow and arrow, his horse was disciplined to respond to his voice, the shifting of his hips, and the pressure of his knees. A truly skilled hunter could send an arrow clean through a buffalo, emerging on the animal's far side. Each arrow had a long, tapered head, with its rear sloping backward, which made it all the better to recover and reuse. A groove along the shaft would allow the buffalo's blood to flow freely, helping the fallen animal to bleed to death.

The finest American Indian buffalo slayers were men of great patience, guile, and speed, rather than brute power. They displayed traits honed from birth—the gifts of a caring, close-knit tribe.

BRAVE AS AN ELK

Among the Sioux, a child was considered to have been sent by *Wakan Tanka*, the Great Spirit, as a precious gift, to be treasured not only by his biological parents but also by the community as a whole. "Every fire became like that of his parents, welcoming the exploring, the sleepy, or injured toddler," Mari Sandoz notes. "Every pot would have a little extra for a hungry boy, and every ear was open to young sorrow, young joys and aspirations."

So it was with Slow when, as a child, he sought to know and explore the world around him. As a Hunkpapa infant, he would have been taught to swim almost from birth. "After all," as Sandoz points out, "every Indian child had to keep himself afloat awhile if he slipped off into deep water, was caught in a cloudburst or in a river accident while the people were fleeing enemies or a buffalo stampede."

As Slow grew, his father impressed upon him the need to study the animals and model himself after them. According to Albert Marrin, "He should be brave as an elk, watchful as the frog, patient as the spider, quiet as the snake, swift as the dragonfly, elusive as the coyote, and strong as a buffalo." A boy would be taught to pick up animal droppings, feel them, their hardness and warmth telling him what animal had left them, what it had eaten, and how close it was. He even learned to "read" a patch of dried urine. "The position of urine in relation to a horse's hoof prints revealed its sex and its rider's mission," Marrin notes.

It was, of course, a kinship with horses that Slow, above all else, was expected to establish at an early age. At three, he could probably mount a horse, even if it meant shinnying up the animal's foreleg, as a squirrel ascends a tree. At five, Slow would probably have been given his own horse to care for. By the age of seven, he was undoubtedly looking after the family herd.

And at the age of 10, Slow killed his first buffalo. "When I was ten years old," Slow later boasted, according to Robert Utley, "I was famous as a hunter. My specialty was buffalo calves. I gave the calves that I killed to the poor that had no horses. I was considered a good man."

By the time Slow reached his teens, he was clearly an accomplished horseman. Slow, no doubt, had learned to ride hour upon hour at the fastest speed. He would have been taught to leap from a tired horse to a fresh mount while both were at full gallop. Slow, most assuredly, even learned to sleep while riding. According to Thomas Mails, "Groups would divide into sections while being pursued, one section sleeping hanging over their horse's necks, while the other led them—and drove a stolen herd at the same time."

Thus, at the age of 14 when Slow was given his new name, Sitting Bull, he had learned and absorbed much. A Hunkpapa hunter/warrior, provider/protector, of extraordinary promise had emerged.

THE LAKOTA WAY

The mid- to late-nineteenth-century Lakota-Sioux were the quintessential Plains Indians of our contemporary imagination. Feather-strewn, yet nearly naked, the horseback-riding hunter/warrior Lakota are, thanks to cheap novels and Hollywood movies, what most Americans see when they envision American Indians of the Old West. Nonetheless, in counterpoint to this warring, violent image, the Lakota lived a life built on comforting family values and, above all, spirituality. The Lakota were a deeply religious people, forever seeking a oneness with *Wakan Tanka*, the Great Mystery.

Central to understanding the all-encompassing Wakan Tanka was the belief in the "circle of life." According to William Wallis, author of *Selected Essays*, "Through his [the Lakota's] words he expresses his fundamental belief: that all life is a circle of being and that all things belong in that circle. He seeks harmony with the forces of nature so that he might become one with them, one with the Great Mystery, which is all things."

For the Lakota, the circle was everywhere. His home, the tepee, was circular. When setting up camp, tepees were placed in a circle. Celestial objects, such as the Sun and the Moon, were, of course, circular. To the Lakota, all good and natural things were circular in form. For them, it was about wishing to be one with the world, to reside, as Wallis declared, "with the whole circle of existence."

The Sun Dance was a religious ceremony common to the American Indian tribes of the Great Plains. Dancing to honor their connection to the Great Spirit (or as the Lakota called it, the "Great Mystery"), these tribes would gather in a circle and sing, dance, fast, experience visions, and sometimes men would self-mutilate as a religious offering.

In seeking accord with *Wakan Tanka*, the Lakota gathered annually for the Sun Dance, which was performed in a great circle. The most sacred of all Lakota ceremonies, the Sun Dance was held for 12 days around the time of the summer solstice. The dance involved singing, dancing, drumming, fasting, and the seeking of a vision. It also embraced self-mutilation. According to Albert Marrin, "Men (but never women) offered their flesh and blood to show gratitude for past blessings and to gain wisdom for the future. This ceremony grew out of the belief that all things came forth in pain." Thus, for a Lakota male, in performing self-sacrifice he was giving, literally, part of himself to *Wakan Tanka*, the only thing that was truly his to offer. As Lakota tribe member, Chase-by-Bears, told it, "I must give something that I really value. . . . Therefore I promise to give my whole body."

Beyond the overall infusion of spirituality into the life of every Lakota, males sought to live their lives through the expression of four cardinal virtues. The ideals of bravery, fortitude, generosity, and wisdom represented goals a Lakota man was expected to cultivate and practice. The first three were virtues Sitting Bull developed and amply displayed as he grew from childhood to early manhood. Sitting Bull would acquire the fourth, wisdom, in time. When he did, it would make him a true leader, a great chief, and perhaps the most revered and respected American Indian of all time.

COUNTING COUPS

Of the four virtues, bravery took first rank. A warrior who risked his life to save a comrade showed the highest form of heroism. Such individual valor meant more than group victory; slaying an enemy up close, when counting coup, was more impressive than taking him down from afar. In a society in which the warrior was praised above all, in which defense of the tribe was paramount, it is only natural that bravery would be valued so highly.

The model for bravery could be found, as with so many things in a Sioux's world, by examining nature and by studying the animals that roamed the Plains. Here the fighting qualities of the buffalo impressed the Lakota Sioux most. "Everyone knew that the buffalo was a headstrong, stubborn creature, afraid of nothing," Stanley Vestal reported. "It never turned back, never gave up, no matter what the obstacle, but always kept on going ahead, whatever the danger, whatever the weather. . . . It was all endurance, headstrong courage, persistence, and strength." Such was a fitting model for a youthful

Sitting Bull. As he grew to adulthood, he would imitate the buffalo over any man.

From childhood, aspiring warriors were trained to never show cowardice, to always demonstrate bravery. Such young men were constantly placed in situations in which their courage and alertness would be tested. If a boy failed to live up to expectations, to demonstrate the bravery expected of a future warrior and hunter, he would often be ostracized. In some tribes, he would be required to put on women's clothing and live as a woman.

Perhaps the greatest expression of bravery came with counting coup. To count coup meant to inflict a blow on an enemy. In times long ago, a Sioux fought at close quarters, in hand-to-hand combat; he had no choice. Even when long-range weapons were developed, such as the bow and arrow and the lance, the Sioux still regarded combat up close as the only truly manly way to fight. He wanted, above all, to strike his enemy with his hand or with something in his hand; doing so often entailed great risks.

Walloping an enemy was the goal of every warrior. Counting coup meant the most in battle. When a warrior struck a foe, he would often yell, "I have overcome this one," to alert a witness who could testify to the deed. Later honors would be bestowed on the man, and he would have the right to narrate his feat at any public gathering.

Early on, Sitting Bull began to garner coups. Before the age of 21, he may have amassed a half-dozen. In one instance, when a Crow foe ran out of arrows, Sitting Bull, having three, threw down two within reach of his enemy. As the Crow placed a fallen arrow in his bowstring, Sitting Bull shot him dead with his remaining arrow. "*Tatan'ka Iyotaq'ke he miye*—Sitting Bull, I am he," the young Hunkpapa shouted, according to Albert Marrin. Sitting Bull loved a fight.

VISION QUEST

Fortitude, the strength of mind that enables one to encounter danger, bear pain, or face adversity with fearlessness, was the second most sought-after virtue for all Lakota. At its most obvious, fortitude was the ability to endure physical distress and discomfort. Being able to withstand the brutal freezing winters of the northern Plains demonstrated one's fortitude. The courage to handle the scalding steam of a sweat lodge demanded fortitude. Being able to suffer the wounds of an enemy arrow required fortitude. Above all, the capacity to tolerate the personal sacrifices of the Sun Dance, without any visible sign of distress, was the ultimate reflection of a male Lakota's courage, mettle, pluck, and pure grit.

Before a Lakota man sought to participate in a Sun Dance (around the age of 20), he was expected to have undergone a *hanblecheya*, or "crying out for a vision." The hanblecheya can be thought of as a pre-Sun Dance experience, a way to prepare for the "main event" of the Sun Dance.

In seeking his vision, an adolescent was required to fast alone for four days in a remote location, without clothing or shelter, all the time praying for a sign from the spirits. According to Robert Utley:

> The vision usually appeared to him objectified in a patron animal or bird. Somewhere between the ages of ten and fourteen, the boy solicited counsel and instruction from a holy man, purified himself in a sweat lodge, and went to a remote hill to fast and struggle until the vision came. Afterward, the holy man interpreted the vision and helped devise a special fetish or design to summon the power when needed.

Once obtained, the vision was to equip the youth with a great guiding power to help him through life. While there is no direct evidence of Sitting Bull's youthful vision quest, there can be little doubt that he underwent one. Because such a vision was profoundly personal, it is understandable that Sitting Bull would not have shared the experience with anyone but the *Wichasha Wakan* (holy man) who helped him prepare for the vision and later interpret it.

Centaurs of the Plains

The dictionary defines *centaur* as a mythical monster having the head, torso, and arms of a man, and the body and legs of a horse. The term also refers to a skillful horseman or horsewoman. When it came to expertise on horseback, the Plains Indians took second place to no one, not even the famed Arabs or the Cossacks of Asia.

Louis S. Warren offers a vivid description of what the *wasichu* (the white man) thought of American Indian horsemen and the many characteristics they displayed. Writing in *Buffalo Bill's America: William Cody and the Wild West Show,* the author declares:

> Cavalrymen, who venerated great horsemanship, were astounded at Cheyenne, Lakota, and other Indians who galloped bareback amid stampeding buffalo, firing continuous streams of arrows without putting hand to reins. In warfare, their horsecraft was awesome. Hooking one heel over a horse's back, they clung to the sides of their mounts and used animals' bodies as shields from enemy fire, and the showier of men even returned fire from under their horse's necks. . . . One shocked officer reported that a Cheyenne brave scooped up a soldier's corpse at full gallop, stripped him naked . . . and discarded the body—without even slowing down.

Plains Indians—the true centaurs of the West.

Although fortitude meant the ability to withstand pain, for the Lakota it was more than that. A man demonstrated fortitude, as well, by exhibiting a high degree of dignity and reserve, especially with regard to emotional distress. Above all, excitement, affection, and humor needed to be kept in reserve, lest they be unduly displayed to strangers, particularly the white man.

GIVEAWAYS

Generosity is a virtue demanded by any interdependent community, with the Lakota and all the Plains Indian tribes being no exception. Unselfishness reflected the understanding that it was people and not things that counted. Property existed in the Lakota world, of course, with the possession of many horses elevating an owner in the eyes of all community members. But it was when such a holder gave away his horses to orphans, the crippled, and the old that his prestige soared. If you had more than one of anything, the Lakota principle went, you should give the rest away.

Along with generosity went honesty, an absolute in any Lakota community. As Mari Sandoz succinctly put it, "A society that has no locks can tolerate no thief; without paper or other easy record of man's word, it can tolerate no liar; and no troublemaker if there is no jail, no prison." As a consequence, people had no hesitancy in leaving goods unattended. A lost piece of property would be immediately delivered to the camp crier, who would carry it throughout the camp, asking to whom it belonged.

Food within the tribe was always shared. Except in times of great hardship and scarcity, something to eat was anyone's for the asking. Every visitor received his share without hesitation.

Friendship, of course, was a reflection of generosity. Childhood fellowships often lasted a lifetime. For a "best friend," it was expected that one would lay down his life in times of battle or special need.

Tom Newcomb, a scout for General Nelson Miles in the early 1870s, and one who later lived with the Sioux, stated, according to Thomas Mails, "that he never saw more kindness, charity, and brotherhood anywhere than he did among the Sioux."

In Sitting Bull's tenth year, an incident occurred that not only demonstrated his already acquired skill with a bow and arrow, but also the emerging characteristic of generosity.

One day, while on shooting practice with other boys of his tribe, Slow, who was not yet called Sitting Bull, sought to hit an oriole, one of the hardest birds to target with a bow and arrow. A fellow hunter, one who was a notorious bully, shot first but missed, lodging his arrow in a tree limb. He offered the prize of one of his best arrows if someone could retrieve his stuck arrow. Using a special blunt-pointed arrow, Slow took careful aim and hit the lost arrow, knocking it to the ground but also shattering it. The furious owner demanded that Slow pay for the broken arrow. After a heated argument, Slow declared, as quoted by Robert Utley, "Here, take my blunt-point arrow that caused you so much grief. Keep it and get your bird." If it was not for Slow's magnanimous act, trouble might have ensued.

THE WISE MAN

With enough hard work, practice, and dedication, a Lakota man could master the first three virtues of bravery, fortitude, and generosity by the time he was in his mid-twenties. The fourth virtue, that of wisdom, not only took longer, but it also came to only a few. According to William Wallis:

> Wisdom for the Lakota implies far more than just intelligence. It implies power from the supernatural. . . . Wisdom involves the ability to get along with others, to arbitrate disputes, to instill confidence as a leader of war parties or as an advisor of young men. Those who are truly wise perform the sacred ceremonies. They are thought to have the power of helping others and their word comes as if from the spirits.

The Lakota taught their youth the basis of wisdom through the many admonishments they would recite. For example, a boy might be told that he should not eat a particular soft part of the buffalo otherwise his legs might become soft. Of course, that would not happen, but the youth was, through this chastisement, being shown how to be courteous to the elders among him, leaving the soft parts for them to more easily chew.

A young person also was cautioned to never pass between a camp or tepee fire and someone else, lest he cut that person off, even momentarily, from the fire's warmth.

In the mid-nineteenth century, weary Easterners packed up their belongings in covered wagons and headed into the rugged western frontier to establish new lives. Traveling along routes like the Oregon Trail (*above*), these large groups of settlers were often seen by American Indians as an ominous sign of American expansion into Native territories.

Etiquette required that a person's name not be mentioned in his presence. According to Thomas Mails, "Others were addressed as father, mother, friend, brother, etc. These were terms of relationships which express a love that is not conveyed when the personal name is used. The American Indians felt that any impersonal stranger could use a name. In the same way, a man of standing would be called 'aged man,' which granted him the status of wisdom and which tended to bring forth a profound response."

In time, Sitting Bull would be considered a man of great wisdom, a supreme holy man. "Few surpassed him in bravery, fortitude, or generosity, and none, so long as the old ways lasted, in wisdom," Utley declared. "He represented the ideal to which all aspired."

As the *wasichu*, or white man, encroached ever more menacingly on the land of the Sioux in the mid-nineteenth century, Sitting Bull's wisdom and leadership would be required more than ever.

WASICHU CHALLENGE

The Cherokee called it *Nunna dual Tsuny*, or "The Trail of Tears." Sixteen thousand of them, part of an eastern American Indian tribe that had prospered in Tennessee for more than 100 years, were now, on a bright May day in 1838, to be forcibly transported 1,200 miles (1,930 kilometers) to lands west of the Mississippi River, across the supposed "permanent Indian frontier."

A military force of 7,000, under the command of General Winfield Scott, was commissioned to gather up the Cherokee (many of whom had learned to read and write, run their own sawmills, and build sturdy houses) for the long march out of the East, where white settlers had demanded their removal. "Every possible kindness . . . must be shown by the troops," Scott had declared the day before, as reported in *Indian Wars*. "And, if, in the ranks, a despicable individual should be found, capable of inflicting a wanton injury or insult on any Cherokee man, woman, or child, it is hereby made the special duty of the nearest good officer or man, instantly to interpose, and to seize and consign the guilty wretch to the severest penalty of the laws."

In the roundup that took place, where Cherokees by the thousand were penned up in concentration camps before the actual

The relocation of the American Indians from the eastern United States to west of the Mississippi River is commonly referred to as the Trail of Tears. A British treaty declared that a swath of land from the Appalachian Mountains to the Mississippi River was originally American Indian land, but U.S. expansion led to the removal of an estimated 100,000 American Indians from various tribes including the Cherokee, Seminole, and Choctaw.

march, many died and fell ill from the stifling summer heat. Some were raped, others robbed, and some murdered. Whites looted their homes as many American Indians were dragged, at bayonet, into confinement. Then, in the late autumn and early winter, contingents started west, some on wagons, some on foot, some in flatboats. The Trail of Tears had begun.

When it was finally over, and the remaining Cherokees had crossed the gray, swollen Mississippi, they could look back at 4,000 graves littering their trail. One out of four had died of cold, hunger, or disease on their way west.

The forced march of 1838 ended the American Indian "menace" east of the Mississippi River once and for all. According to Dee Brown, author of *Bury My Heart at Wounded Knee*, scattered or reduced to remnants were,

> Pequots, Montauks, Nanticokes, Machapungas, Catawbas, Cheraws, Miamis, Hurons, Eries, Mohawks, Senecas, and Mohegans. . . . Their musical names remained forever fixed on the American land, but their bones were forgotten in a thousand burned villages or lost in forests fast disappearing before the axes of twenty million invaders.

The Cherokee would now occupy the land of the proud and free Plains Indians. The United States government assured them that they would finally be safe, away from land-grabbing whites. Such whites would not cross in any great numbers onto the Great Plains, the Cherokee were told. After all, the dry, flat land was referred to then as the Great American Desert—a godforsaken place fit only for American Indians.

WESTWARD HO

Of course, the *wasichu* did not stop at the Mississippi River, or even the new "permanent Indian frontier," when it was moved a few hundred miles to the west, to the 95th meridian, a line of longitude that passes through Minnesota and all the way down to Texas. Most still saw the Plains as unattractive for general settlement. This was particularly true when the vast region, with little timber and surface water, was compared to the fertile lands, big rivers, and seaports of far-off Oregon.

Getting to Oregon, however, was not easy. By the early 1840s, if one chose to cross the continent, a five- to six-month journey through hostile Indian Territory was required. Traveling what became known, logically enough, as the Oregon Trail, pioneers and settlers would usually leave Elm Grove, Missouri in the east, and travel west through the future states of Missouri, Kansas, Nebraska, Wyoming, Idaho, and Oregon. In 1843, an estimated 1,000 immigrants, led by Marcus Whitman, set out in what was dubbed the "Wagon Train of 1843." Hundreds of thousands more were soon to follow, especially after gold was discovered in California in 1848.

Plains Indians, particularly the Lakota, were not pleased with what was happening. "Indians who lived or hunted along the Santa Fe and Oregon trails had grown accustomed to seeing an occasional wagon train licensed for traders, trappers, or missionaries," Dee Brown noted. "Now suddenly the trails were filled with wagons, and the wagons were filled with white people. Most of them were bound for California gold, but some turned southwest for New Mexico or northwest for the Oregon country."

From the American Indian point of view, it would only get worse. "By 1843, the road shoulders on both sides of the North Platte and Sweetwater sections of the Oregon Trail were virtually devoid of grass—and wagon traffic west had only just begun," wrote the authors of the Web site *Native American Tribes*. "The buffalo were scared off, the meager stands of river-bottom timber were depleted, and streambeds were made muddy from cattle tracks."

It wasn't long before bands of Lakota warriors were stopping wagon trains and demanding payment to travel through their territory. In turn, the travelers were quick to request help from their government for protection in the form of forts and soldiers. The foundation for serious conflict was at hand.

Finally, when the Treaty of Guadalupe Hidalgo ended the Mexican-American War in 1848 (while adding more than 500,000 square miles, or 1.3 million sq. km, to the United States), the "permanent Indian frontier" simply dissolved. As Robert Utley observed, "By Sitting Bull's twentieth birthday, in 1851, the United States had flung its western boundary to the Pacific and swelled to a continental nation of 23.2 million people and 3 million square miles [7.7 million square km]."

With Manifest Destiny, the belief God gave Americans the right to expand across the continent, in full force, and with Plains Indian tribes harassing white travelers as well as fighting among themselves, it became the responsibility of the U.S. government to make the Plains a safer place for its citizens. An agreement of some sort to pacify the people was an urgent necessity.

PEACE TALKERS

It was the largest gathering of Plains Indian tribes ever. From the north came the Blackfeet and Crow. From the west, the Shoshone arrived. Out of the northeast came the Arikara, Hitatsa, and Mandan. From the south streamed the Arapaho, and, of course, the mighty Cheyenne. Since what would be called the Great Indian Treaty Council at Fort Laramie, in Wyoming Territory, was within Lakota territory, there were Hunkpapa as well. The Pawnees (bitter enemies of the Sioux), however, refused to come. According to Robert Utley and Wilcomb Washburn, "The Pawnees had too many horses and mules to risk . . . among such notorious horse thieves as the Sioux and the Crow."

Though many tribes found themselves deep within enemy territory, curiosity about the wasichu brought them together in common purpose. For weeks after the initial arrivals began to gather in the summer of 1851, there would be horse racing, dancing, trading, and much merry-making. "Contributing to the general noise and commotion," the authors of *Native American Tribes* wrote, "were hundreds of dogs, some of which would serve as prized delicacies in the feasting ahead."

The sea of tepees, stretching to the horizon, represented no less than 10,000 families from nine Plains Indian tribes. They had all come, as Joseph Marshall III declared, "to listen to the *wolakotiye woglakapi*, or 'peace talkers,' of the whites, as the Lakota understood them to be."

Listening, however, turned out to be difficult, what with nine languages and various subdialects in play. But the gist of what the whites wanted was apparent when it came time to put pen to paper and sign, or write X's, on a treaty document. In effect, on September 17, 1851, in what would come to be known as the first Fort Laramie Treaty, old enemies lined up to do the white man's bidding. In

Officials from the U.S. government and representatives of the various American Indian tribes of the Great Plains negotiated and agreed on the terms of the Fort Laramie Treaty of 1851. Although most of the American Indians in attendance agreed to stop raiding wagon trains, there were some (including Sitting Bull's tribe, the Hunkpapa) that refused to sign the treaty and continued to attack traveling settlers.

signing the treaty, all agreed, at least as far as the U.S. government was concerned, to do three things: one, they would respect one another's boundaries—that is, stop fighting among themselves; two, all tribes would refrain from harassing settlers on the Oregon Trail; and, three, the American Indians would allow new roads and military posts to be built on their lands.

In return for all this peacemaking, the American Indians would be allowed to hunt and fish at will within their designated territories. And, just as important, they would receive annual payments from

Sioux Warfare

Why did the Sioux fight? Why were they a warrior society? Clearly the Sioux, and in particular the Lakota, were widely recognized for their strength in warfare. They wished to fight and they fought well.

According to Guy Gibbon, in his excellent book *The Sioux: The Dakota and the Lakota Nations*, "As in other Plains Indian nomadic societies, Sioux warfare was essentially an individual enterprise, with small-scale war parties organized without the sanction of larger social units." In other words, battles often took place at the whim of a few, usually young, "hothead" males looking to advance up the social ladder. Gibbon continues, "Conflicts tended to be brief, indecisive surprise attacks, fought more for glory and horses than to exterminate the foe. Counting coup and other valorous deeds usually took precedence over slaying enemies. Few large-scale battles were fought, formally organized fighting units were rare, and long campaigns by large forces were seldom engaged in for logistic reasons."

Even if the Lakota fought mostly for immediate, personal reasons, there can be little doubt that the encroachment of whites, competition for good hunting grounds, the warfare-revenge cycle, and a general fear of outsiders played a part as well. Clearly, both psychological and broader economic, political, and social causes worked to make the Lakota and all Plains Indian tribes warrior societies.

the government in the form of goods, such as tobacco, kettles, and blankets, worth $50,000 per year for 15 years—a paltry sum, even when valued at about $1.2 million in today's dollars.

It is doubtful that many leaders who signed the treaty understood its details. At the mighty gathering, the government had offered $100,000 worth of presents to make signing more palatable. Significantly, though, the Hunkpapa did not sign. By the end of the year, old hostilities between ancient American Indian enemies would resume.

The Fort Laramie Treaty of 1851 can be seen as the beginning of a major schism that would divide not only the Hunkpapa, but all Plains Indians in the years ahead. There would be those, mostly older members of a tribe, who would be attracted by the government annuities, or the annual payments in goods that they would become more and more dependent upon. They would favor peace.

At the same time, younger men, who had no patience with peace talks, who believed that war offered the only path to honor, status, and rank, insisted that they should pursue, as their fathers had before them, the gathering of scalps and horses. At 20 years old, Sitting Bull clearly fell into this camp, one filled with hotheaded zealots out for war honors.

STRONG HEARTS

As an exalted warrior with his teenage years behind him, Sitting Bull had, in the early 1850s, no trouble being accepted into the numerous Hunkpapa fraternal organizations celebrating warfare, such as the Strong Hearts Society. The Strong Hearts, an elite group among such braves, swore never to retreat in war. They would often stake themselves to the ground during a battle to emphasize the point.

In combat, Sitting Bull had been distinguishing himself since the age of 14, when he garnered his first coup. The Hunkpapa warrior, however, did not go entirely unscathed in his numerous enemy encounters. In 1856, in a fight with the Crows, Sitting Bull earned his second red feather, a badge signifying a wound in battle. In the struggle, he would sustain an injury that would bother him the rest of his life.

High up on the Yellowstone River, the Crows faced the Hunkpapa, who had just stolen some of their finest horses. A Crow chief called upon Sitting Bull, challenging him to a duel with the trade muskets each were holding in their hands. Quickly, the two crouched and fired. Sitting Bull's shot was true, his ball hitting the chief in the belly, killing him. But the Crow's ball punched through Sitting Bull's shield, striking his upturned foot and tearing a groove from toe to heel. That night, Sitting Bull could not dance in the victory dance. He would walk with a pronounced limp for the rest of his life.

Sitting Bull, of course, lost no status as a result of his foot injury. Indeed, a year later, in 1857, the Strong Hearts Society made him a war chief. Soon after, he became war chief of the entire Hunkpapa tribe.

That same year, Sitting Bull demonstrated, in a most convincing manner, that being war chief of the Hunkpapas not only meant leading in battle, but showing genuine compassion upon occasion.

In a battle with the Assiniboine, a young enemy boy of 13 got caught up in the clash. The boy had tried to defend himself, but his arrow had slipped from his bow string. As he was about to be killed by Swift Cloud and other Hunkpapa, the youth, according to Robert Utley, "cried and turned to Sitting Bull, threw his arms around him, and called him 'older brother.' Touched, Sitting Bull declared that the boy should be spared."

Sitting Bull's new brother would remain loyal to his savior for the rest of the chief's life. For a time, he would be called Hohe, or Stays Back, because he refused to return to his people when given the chance.

DEATH OF A FATHER

Jumping Bull, Sitting Bull's father, was in great agony from being in extreme pain. It was June 1859, and the chief's jaw had, over the past few days, swollen to twice its normal size. With the gentlest touch, a "bolt of lightning" blasted through his skull. Jumping Bull would rock back and forth in his tepee, his toothache gnawing at him. At 60 years of age, Sitting Bull's father was getting old. His teeth were deteriorating. He told those around him that he wanted to die. Tragically, the next day he would get his wish.

As the sun rose and the Hunkpapa band of warriors left their camp, they were immediately put upon by more than 50 Crow. After prolonged fighting, Sitting Bull and his men drove them off in a fierce counterattack. In the pursuit that followed, however, a Crow's horse went lame. Jumping Bull, though well beyond the age where he might be expected to engage in combat, dismounted and took aim with his raised bow and arrow. The Crow shot first, however, and Jumping Bull fell, mortally wounded. Not content with his death deed, however, the Crow raced forward and plunged a knife into the top of Jumping Bull's head, snapping the blade from the handle as he did.

Sitting Bull, having been summoned, raced to the scene of his father's death. With not even a second glance, he reared up and pursued the Crow slayer, stabbing him with a lance. That was not enough for Sitting Bull, however; in his rage, he hacked the Crow to pieces, tossing his body parts over his shoulder.

That night, three captured Crow women were brought before Sitting Bull. Everyone expected the chief to order their execution, but in a compassionate gesture the Hunkpapa leader said no. "It is not right," he declared, as reported by Albert Marrin. "Treat them well, and let them live. My father was a man and death is his."

The next day Sitting Bull gave his father's name away—to Hohe, his new brother.

DETERMINED FOE

As a young Lakota boy growing into manhood, having already demonstrated bravery and fortitude in the hunt and in the battle, one walked among his fellows with confidence. Not so, however, with the opposite sex. Here, even the toughest Hunkpapa braggart was often reduced to a shy mute.

Referring to the great Sioux warriors, Crazy Horse and his life-long friend, He Dog, Mari Sandoz relates a revealing story:

> Although both had killed their buffalo and counted coups in battle as boys along on war parties, almost the same day the two were struck with a burning self-consciousness when a girl looked at them. Suddenly they were too bashful to go stand at the water path as usual, too tongue-tied to speak to the girls who had been in the games, the swims, the berryings for years, the girls they had teased and shouted to as casually as all the others only a few days ago.

Of Sitting Bull's courting there is scant record. Given his admired attributes, however, there is little doubt that he was quite a lady's man. In 1851, the 20-year-old Hunkpapa took the first of what would be five wives. Her name was Light Hair, though some also referred to her as Pretty Door.

As newlyweds, Sitting Bull and Light Hair would often go on hunting trips together. One day, while camped where the Powder River flows into the Yellowstone, a Crow warrior snuck up on them. Light Hair saw the Crow's reflection in the soup she was stirring and, without looking up, alerted her husband. Sitting Bull lifted his bow and shot the intruder. Though the Crow escaped, he left a blood trail that told the composed husband that his arrow had hit its target.

With such a close marriage, it is a mystery why, in 1856, Sitting Bull chose to take advantage of his tribe's practice of polygamy, where a man could have more than one wife, to bring a second woman into his tepee. Her name was Snow on Her, and she was not about to play second drum to Light Hair. "Snow on Her would not act in a sisterly manner," Stanley Vestal reported. "She would not take orders from Light Hair, nor meekly go to bed by herself while her husband snuggled under the buffalo robes with Light Hair across the lodge."

Indeed, the three slept side by side. It seems Sitting Bull would lie on his back, with one wife clinging to his arm and leg on one side, while the other did the same on the opposite flank. Poor Sitting Bull never got comfortable enough to get a good night's sleep, awaking each morning with muscles so cramped and sore that he could hardly walk.

Sitting Bull, in taking a second wife, had obviously made a serious miscalculation. Eventually, Snow on Her was banished from the warrior's tepee and moved back with her parents. When, in 1857, Light Hair died in childbirth, however, Snow on Her returned to Sitting Bull. In the years ahead, the two would have two children, Many Horse, born in 1863, and Walks Looking, in 1868.

KILLDEER MOUNTAIN

In the decade following the Fort Laramie Treaty of 1851, the Plains Indians continued to harass one another and, occasionally, white travelers, irrespective of the pledge to remain peaceful. The wasichu, engaging in their own massive intertribal conflict, the Civil War (1861–1865), found it difficult (though not impossible) to deal aggressively with the "hostiles" out west. Not so, however, in coping

Years after the Fort Laramie Treaty of 1851 was signed, it was clear that both sides were not respecting the agreement. With settlers pouring into American Indian territory and occupying more land, combined with a bad harvest and starving families, the Dakota Sioux in Minnesota initiated an uprising that was stopped by the U.S. military. When it was over, 38 Dakota Sioux warriors were hanged for their participation in the conflict (*above*).

with the more "pacified" American Indians farther east, in the lakes of Minnesota.

On August 17, 1862, a group of young Dakota Sioux murdered five settlers near Acton, Minnesota. The Dakota, having suffered grievously under white "management," had simply had enough. In response to the Sioux "uprising," the state militia of Minnesota, led by Henry Hastings Sibley, gathered 1,500 soldiers, who tangled with the Indians in a number of skirmishes, culminating in the Battle of Wood Lake, on September 23. The conflict, known as the Santee War, inflicted a major defeat on the Dakota. As a consequence, American Indian refugees poured out of Minnesota, heading west into Nakota and Lakota territories. The migration would set in motion conflicts between the wasichu and the Lakota that would last a generation.

Encroachment of *wasichu* onto Lakota lands, steady and sure from before the Fort Laramie Treaty and on into the early 1860s, suddenly developed into a stampede with the discovery of gold in the Rocky Mountains in 1862. The Lakota responded with numerous attacks on white settlers and those heading to the mines to dig for the precious metal.

In July 1864, events came to a head when the Hunkpapa fought U.S. soldiers in what would be one of the biggest conflicts of the northern Plains, the Battle of Killdeer Mountain.

Sitting Bull, now a married 33-year-old war chief, would be fully immersed in the fight. He was not at all concerned as to what might happen or how well his warriors would do in a battle with the enemy. In an uncharacteristic display of poor judgment, the Hunkpapa leader underestimated the bluecoats his men were soon to face. "The white soldiers do not know how to fight," he declared, as reported by Bill Yenne in *Sitting Bull*. "They are not lively enough. They stand still and run straight; it is easy to shoot them. They do not try to save themselves. Also, they seem to have no hearts. When an Indian gets killed, the other Indians feel sorry and cry, and sometimes stop fighting. But when a white soldier gets killed, nobody cries, nobody cares; they go right on shooting and let him lie there. Sometimes they even go off and leave their wounded behind them."

So confident was Sitting Bull when he rode forth to engage soldiers at Killdeer Mountain, he failed to take the precaution of ordering Hunkpapa lodges packed or the village moved. In fact, women, children, and old men gathered on a nearby hill to watch what they assumed would be a great victory. Instead, they witnessed a stunning defeat at the hands of U.S. Army General Alfred Sully.

The Hunkpapa fought bravely, but their feeble weapons were no match for the soldiers' six-shooter revolvers, rifles, and cannons. The bluecoats scattered Hunkpapa women and children into the mountains and set their village on fire, destroying everything the Indians depended on—meat, robes, utensils, and even the lodges

Bows and Arrows

Writing in his monumental work, *The Mystic Warriors of the Plains,* Thomas E. Mails said of the American Indian bow and arrow:

Popular opinion had regarded the Indian bow and arrow as something primitive and well enough for the pursuit of game, but quite useless in a contest with the white man. This idea would be excellent if the Indian warriors would calmly march up in the line of battle and risk their masses so armed among others armed with the rifle. But the Indian comes as a hornet comes, in clouds or singly, yet never trying to sting until his ascending is assured and his own exposure is slight. At fifty yards a well-shapen, non-pointed arrow is dangerous and very sure. A handful drawn from a quiver and discharged successively will make a more rapid fire than that of the revolver, and at very short range will farther penetrate a piece of plank or timber than the ball of an ordinary Colts' navy pistol.

For the would-be Plains Indian warrior, the first childhood plaything was often a miniature bow and a few blunt arrows. Little boys often obtained an uncanny degree of accuracy when shooting at rolling hoops or birds in flight. According to Mails, "They could even spin around and hit pennies inserted in a split stick which was placed fifteen or more feet away from them."

themselves. Sitting Bull, who had admonished the U.S. Army to send men, not women, to fight him, was forced to revise his estimation of the *wasichu* force his people now faced.

SAND CREEK MASSACRE

The Lakota were not the only targets of military wrath, as western settlers and miners sought protection from other aggressive American Indians who, in turn, felt ever more squeezed by the wasichu presence. During the Civil War, the Cheyenne, in eastern Colorado, took advantage of the lack of military personnel out west to raid wagon trains, stagecoach lines, and mining camps. Finally, in early 1864, with whites in the Colorado Territory out to punish any and all American Indians, the territorial governor, John Evans, found little trouble in quickly raising a volunteer force of 700 to quell what he saw as ever-increasing violence.

The governor chose an able troop commander in Colonel John Chivington, a man who once belonged to the clergy, to lead an offensive against the American Indians. Although perhaps a compassionate man among his own kind, any empathy the former Methodist preacher harbored was in no way extended to the Native Peoples. "Damn any man who sympathizes with Indians," Dee Brown reported the colonel declaring. "I have come to kill Indians and believe it is right and honorable to use any means under God's heaven to kill Indians."

And kill them he did.

Chivington's primary target would be Black Kettle and his band of some 600 Southern Cheyenne, camped at Sand Creek, on a branch of the Arkansas River. Black Kettle was peaceful, the U.S. government having recently declared him friendly. Still, Chivington left Fort Lyon, 40 miles (64 km) south of Sand Creek, in late November determined to annihilate any and all Indians he could find. "Kill and scalp all, big and little," he told his men, as reported by Albert Marrin. "Nits [insect eggs] make lice," the colonel added, referring, of course, to children and babies.

On the morning of November 29, 1864, Chivington and his roughnecks, many of whom were later determined to have been intoxicated, surrounded Black Kettle's village. They quickly mounted four howitzer cannons in strategic locations. Black Kettle, fearing an attack, had posted the U.S. flag as well as the white flag of surrender, over his tepee.

What happened next was a massacre of horrendous proportions. With cannons blasting and rifle fire at its most intense, a hail of hell rained down on the hapless Cheyenne village. The crazed soldiers then charged upon the Cheyenne, killing everyone in

Colonel John M. Chivington, a Methodist clergyman, led a group of volunteer fighters to rid Colorado Territory of American Indians. Chivington led his men to Sand Creek, Colorado, and massacred more than 200 American Indians, many of whom were women and children. Later, when Chivington had six of the men arrested for cowardice in battle, it was revealed that these six men had refused to take part in the bloody event and that many of the volunteer soldiers were drunk.

sight. "They were scalped and their brains knocked out," an interpreter living in the village later declared, as reported in *The Sand Creek Massacre*. "The men used their knives, ripped open women, clubbed little children, knocked them in the head with their rifle butts, beat their brains out, mutilated their bodies in every sense of the word."

In the end, more than 200 Cheyenne were slaughtered at Sand Creek. While easterners, upon hearing of the bloodbath, became outraged, Chivington later appeared in Denver, where he displayed 100 Cheyenne scalps to the delight of his white audience.

Though Sitting Bull and his Lakota were nowhere near Sand Creek during that fateful day in November, the chief took notice of the unprovoked attack. For Sitting Bull (and many other Plains Indian leaders), Sand Creek represented a watershed, a defining moment in the way they would forever view the white man. For the Hunkpapa leader, peace with wasichu soldiers would, from now on, be all but impossible.

THE PIED PIPER SINGS

The wasichu (soldiers and others) just kept coming and coming, all the more so after the Civil War ended in April 1865. The nation could turn its full attention to western expansion, fulfilling its Manifest Destiny.

Whether miners and settlers headed across country to the gold fields and ranch lands of the West Coast or set down stakes along the way, the Plains Indians remained an impediment to their desires and ambitions. At best, Plains Indians were seen as a scary nuisance; at worst, out to scalp every white man, woman, and child lumbering through their territory on covered wagons.

In dealing with the Plains tribes, the U.S. government was of two minds. On the one hand, the Department of the Interior, with its Indian Bureau, took a benevolent, paternalistic attitude. The bureau believed that the Plains Indians could be bought off. Given enough annuities (in the form of food and necessary household utensils) in exchange for peace, the bureau would seek to restrict and pacify the indigenous peoples of the Plains.

The War Department, on the other hand, propagated a more hard-line approach. With plenty of manpower now available (thanks to the ending of the Civil War), the department felt that an aggressive posture was called for. The increase in manpower included "Galvanized Yankees" (captured Confederates who would rather fight Indians than rot in a Union prisoner-of-war camp).

For the next generation, the U.S. government's involvement with Plains Indians would flip-flop between the extremes of peace and war. As Stanley Vestal observed, "So long as the bureau kept on making friendlies out of hostiles, and the Army persisted in making hostiles out of friendlies, neither department could possibly lack employment."

The Plains Indians were also of two minds. Between nations, between tribes, among the Lakota, and even within the Hunkpapa, there were divisions and conflicts, often based on age. The older, more conservative leaders were more willing to sacrifice a certain degree of freedom for annuities. Younger men, those who saw status and recognition through the traditions of hunting and warring, were willing to take nothing from the white man and were more quick to resist.

Among the Lakota, Sitting Bull was clearly of the latter contingent. He saw the Indian Bureau's bribery as degrading. The Lakota leader felt that his people had lived for centuries without U.S. government aid and could continue to do so. While visiting an encampment of "Agency Indians" at Fort Berthold, he told them, according to Bill Yenne, "The United States was sucking them into dependence in order to annihilate them." Then, to underscore his assertion, the Hunkpapa chief dramatically cut himself with a knife, explaining that this was the fate they would receive at General Sully's hands if they gave in to the sweet pied piper song of the Indian Bureau.

THE BATTLE OF FORT RICE

As the *wasichu*, particularly in the northern Plains, kept coming and coming, so, too, did the inevitable army forts and garrisons. Such outposts were used not only to provision and protect white settlers and travelers, but to launch raids on what were perceived as hostile American Indian encampments throughout the Dakota, Wyoming, and Montana territories. Of a particularly intrusive nature, as far as the Lakota were concerned, was Fort Rice, far north along the western bank of the Missouri River in what is now North Dakota.

Fort Rice was never an imposing post. According to Robert Utley, "It [Fort Rice] occupied a grassy flat less than a mile wide, bordered on the east by the river and on all other sides by low hills webbed by ravines that afforded excellent cover for Indians who wanted to approach unseen. A palisade with blockhouses enclosed rude structures fashioned from green cottonwood. The soldiers assigned there held Fort Rice to scarcely more affection than the Sioux."

The Sioux simply wanted the fort destroyed and its inhabitants dispersed or annihilated.

On July 28, 1865, with Sitting Bull in the lead, a band of 300 warriors from several tribes charged Fort Rice from the north, west, and south. While the attackers fought bravely, the U.S. Army prevailed, using their deadly howitzers to lob explosives at concentrations of Indians. Only one U.S. soldier was killed, while the American Indian losses were considerable. For Sitting Bull, the battle was not his finest hour. After the opening charge, the war chief had guided two horses away and then simply took no further action in the battle. According to later informants, as reported by Utley, "This so incensed others of the war expedition that, back in camp, they whipped Sitting Bull and killed the two horses."

That said, Sitting Bull had, nonetheless, succeeded in at least temporarily blocking any peace movement within his Hunkpapa tribe. From now on, he would forever be seen as a leader of the hostiles, American Indians who would not succumb to the temptations of annuities in exchange for the loss of their freedom. Despite the momentary damage to his honor at Fort Rice, Sitting Bull would give no hint of holding back in the years to come. He would lead numerous war expeditions against white soldiers, remaining forever their determined foe.

HOSTILES
AND FRIENDLIES

The *wasichu* just kept coming and coming, all the more so with the discovery of gold near Bannack, Montana, in 1863.

To get to the new mines, seekers of the glittering metal could take the traditional, relatively slow route along the Missouri River. In 1864, however, explorer John M. Bozeman pioneered a new course that cut at an angle northwest from Fort Laramie, across the upper Powder, along the eastern base of the Bighorn Mountains, and on into the western settlements of the recently created Montana Territory. Known as the Bozeman Trail, the shortened path sliced right through treaty-guarded Lakota hunting grounds. In 1866, to safeguard travelers along the Bozeman, the U.S. Army built three new forts, spaced 70 to 90 miles (113 to 145 km) apart. Fort Reno, Fort Phil Kearny, and Fort C.F. Smith would join the already established Fort Laramie as protective military outposts. The Lakota were justifiably outraged.

Sitting Bull was quick to take action, on the northern Missouri. In December 1866, he captured the Fort Buford sawmill, in the process trading shots with troopers at the fort, while the Hunkpapa burned a stockpile of firewood. Sitting Bull moved on to harass crews building Fort Stevenson, downstream from Fort Berthold. In

After the Sand Creek Massacre, American Indians from different tribes and nations of the Great Plains took revenge by attacking settlers and raiding forts and covered wagon trains. Also known as Red Cloud's War, the American Indians discovered the use of decoys and diversionary tactics against U.S. forces. Colonel William Fetterman, though warned about this maneuver, led his men straight into an ambush where they were all killed.

1868, Sitting Bull attacked again, this time going after the crews in Fort Buford's hayfield. Harassment of army troops, in the hopes of shutting down forts along the Bozeman, was a strategy eagerly pursued by the Sioux.

While Sitting Bull was busy with his guerrilla war against Forts Buford and Stevenson in the far north, a 44-year-old Oglala Lakota chief, Red Cloud, with his brilliant military strategist, Crazy Horse, led the fight against the new wasichu intrusions. Ultimately, what became known as Red Cloud's War (1866–1868) would result in a complete victory over U.S. forces and the preservation, albeit temporary, of Lakota control in the Powder River country.

On December 21, 1866, in the most significant battle of the war, Oglala warriors, led by Crazy Horse, attacked Captain William J. Fetterman and his 80 soldiers on a search party out of Fort Phil Kearny. They slaughtered every one of them, including their commander. Ironically, Fetterman had earlier boasted that, as quoted in *Native American Tribes*, "with 80 men I could ride through the Sioux Nation."

Fetterman had been warned not to be deceived by the effective decoy tactics that the Oglalas and their Miniconjous and Cheyenne allies were known to use. Yet when just such a decoy, led by Crazy Horse, appeared along the Lodge Trail Ridge, Fetterman fell for the bait. Perhaps the decoys, standing upon their ponies, lifting their loincloths, and insultingly waggling their bare buttocks at the troopers (in a nineteenth-century version of "mooning") was just too much of a taunt. Fetterman marched over the ridge and down into the Peno Valley, which, with 1,000 to 3,000 American Indians waiting in concealment, turned out to be his, and his men's, Valley of Death.

Forever after known as the Fetterman Massacre by the U.S. government and the Battle of the Hundred Slain by the American Indians, the disaster represented the worst defeat yet for U.S. forces in the West. Though Red Cloud was not present during the Fetterman calamity, he was clearly its inspirational leader. Stunned by the defeat and the fierce resistance Red Cloud was able to muster time and time again, in 1868 the United States was ready to meet the American Indians in council. The government wished to discuss its withdrawal from the "Bloody Bozeman" region.

WE CAN FEED OURSELVES

Red Cloud, having defeated the wasichu soldiers, was prepared to meet and sign a new treaty. He, along with his allies such as American

Horse and Young Man Afraid of His Horses (or They Even Fear His Horses), were ready to accept some form of coexistence—basically a land-for-peace exchange. But not Crazy Horse, and certainly not Sitting Bull. The latter remained on the northern Missouri, determined to resist encroachment and to never accept wasichu annuities. Yet if the white man wanted peace, somehow Sitting Bull and his Hunkpapa war faction would have to be brought on board.

Father Pierre-Jean De Smet (or Black Robe) was chosen as the white man's emissary to the Hunkpapa chief. The priest's mission to Sitting Bull's camp, deep in hostile Indian Territory, could be a dangerous one, not only for him, but his entire contingent. Yet on June 19, 1868, when De Smet entered the Hunkpapa village flying a flag displaying the image of the Virgin Mary, Sitting Bull had the priest's baggage carried into his own tepee. A few hours later, De Smet awoke from a nap to find Sitting Bull crouched beside him.

"Your Grandfather [the American president] wishes you to live among your people on your own lands," Father De Smet told Sitting Bull, as quoted by Stanley Vestal. "You will never starve. You will always have plenty of rations. . . . You will receive warm clothing." In other words, if the Hunkpapa would stop fighting and come live on a reservation set aside for them, they would be taken care of by the Great Father—the United States government. They would have to cease being Hunkpapa Indians as they knew it, but they would survive; they would not be hunted by white soldiers or left to freeze in the dead of winter. Sitting Bull would have none of it.

"It sounds good, but I am satisfied with the old treaty for the hunting tribes if the whites would only keep it," the chief responded to Father De Smet. "Listen my friend, I have a message for the Grandfather. I do not want anyone to bother my people. I want them to live in peace. I myself have plans for my people, and if they follow my plans, they will never want. They will never hunger. I wish for traders only, and no soldiers on my reservation. God gave us this land, and we are at home here. I will not have my people robbed. We can live if we can keep our Black Hills. We do not want to eat from the hand of the Grandfather. We can feed ourselves."

Red Cloud (*left*) and American Horse (*right*) disagreed with Sitting Bull's determined stance against the U.S. government and signed the Fort Laramie Treaty of 1868. Sitting Bull was unwilling to cede any of his people's land to the United States and only wanted the young growing nation to leave the Hunkpapa alone.

Unlike Red Cloud, Sitting Bull was not seeking peaceful coexistence; he only wanted, as he would say many times, to be left alone.

The treaty that was eventually signed on July 2, 1868, at Fort Rice (but known as the Fort Laramie Treaty of 1868), created the "Great Sioux Reservation." The set-aside 22 million acres (8.9 million hectares) would consist of all of what would later become the state of South Dakota west of the Missouri River. Immediately to the west and north of the reservation would be a vast area referred to as "unceded Indian territory." Here, Plains Indians, if they wished, would have the right to, as Article XI of the treaty states, "hunt on any lands north of North Platte . . . so long as buffalo may range thereon in such numbers as to justify the chase." Thus, Sioux who still wished to live by hunting rather than by government handouts might do so. But, as Robert Utley points out, "That neatly postponed a dispute over going to the reservation, but white officials confidently looked to the day when the extinction of the buffalo would eliminate the issue."

Thus, Red Cloud and his followers became "friendlies." They would live on a reservation and accept handouts from the U.S. government. Sitting Bull and his supporters, including the indomitable Crazy Horse, would remain "hostiles." They would stay out altogether, while trying to pursue a hunting and warring life, as they always had. In so doing, Sitting Bull would lead his Lakota Sioux as a newly crowned "itancan-in-chief."

CHIEF SITTING BULL

To effectively lead the opposition to further U.S. expansion into their lands, the Hunkpapa leaders decided to do something unprecedented. In early 1869, the Shirt Wearers, the four-man Hunkpapa executive council, called a conference that involved not only their tribe, but also the Blackfeet, Miniconjous, San Arcs, Oglalas, and Cheyennes. In a truly sweeping scheme, they sought to elect a supreme chief of the Sioux confederation to an "office" that had never existed before. Four Horns, a member of the four-man executive

Bountiful Bison

It is well known that the Plains Indians used every bit of the buffalo, or bison, letting nothing go to waste. Here, from *The Mystic Warriors of the Plains* by Thomas E. Mails, is a partial list of what could be made from this bountiful animal:

From the buffalo's hide: moccasin tops, cradles, winter robes, bedding shirts, belts, pipe bags, quivers, tepee covers, lance covers, dolls, splints, drums, stirrups, bull boats, bullet pouches, armbands, lance cases, and horse masks.

From the buffalo's hair: headdresses, saddle pad fillers, pillows, ropes, ornaments, halters, and medicine balls.

From the buffalo's horns: cups, fire carriers, spoons, ladles, headdresses, and toys.

From the buffalo's muscles and sinew: bows, thread, arrows, cinches, and glue.

From the buffalo's bladder: sinew pouches, quill pouches, and small medicine bags.

From the buffalo's bones: knives, arrowheads, shovels, splints, winter sleds, arrow straighteners, saddle trees, war clubs, scrapers, awls, paintbrushes, and game dice.

---

council and Sitting Bull's uncle, nominated his 38-year-old nephew for the position of "itancan-in-chief."

That Sitting Bull qualified for the leadership role there can be little doubt. "He combined the dynamism and drive of relative youth with experience in war, the hunt, and the political and spiritual leadership of his people," Robert Utley observed. "His war record against enemy tribes ranked with the best. Against the whites, it surpassed all, for in the sustained war against Fort Buford he had truly acted as the Hunkpapa lance, thrusting repeatedly at the soldiers intruding into his homeland. He had been a tribal war chief since 1857 and was active in the men's societies. Of his bravery, despite several troubling episodes, there could be no doubt, nor of the other cardinal virtues either."

Furthermore, that Sitting Bull could, and would, lead by inspiration and example there was no question. He possessed the personal skills all Sioux admired. When the Hunkpapa was presented with a ceremonial pipe, upon his assenting to the chieftainship, "There he sat, that homely cripple, in his plain clothing, and with only two eagle feathers in his hair—one red, in remembrance of his wounds," Stanley Vestal reported. "He had never put on any airs, was never a snob, though pleasantly conscious of his own undoubted merits. . . . He was a man of the people, and never pretended to be anything else."

As supreme chief, it was Sitting Bull's duty to see that his nation was fed, that it had plenty to eat. When their leader said "Fight," the Lakota would do battle. When Sitting Bull said "Make peace," the nation would lay down its bows and arrows.

Crazy Horse was made second in command. Unpretentious and scorning all possessions but his horse and weapons, he was, according to Vestal, "an ideal man for the post." Crazy Horse and Sitting Bull would be the decision makers in every crisis to come. The two would forever remain friends.

It was now time for Sitting Bull to lead the hunting bands, the northern Indians, the hostiles, who would remain in the unceded territory year-round, never to set foot in an agency. For the itancan-in-chief and his wandering people, the road ahead, the one they had chosen, was clear—yet filled with peril.

"SMOKING PARTY"

Of all the intrusions into Lakota lands, the onward press of the white man's iron horse, the railroad, was the most resented. Nowhere was this more so than in the Yellowstone River region, treasured Lakota territory, the tribe's very heartland.

In the fall of 1871, soldiers appeared in the Yellowstone Valley escorting a surveying team for the Northern Pacific Railroad. In

August of the following year, Spotted Eagle, while leading a huge war party of San Arcs and Lakota, with Sitting Bull and Crazy Horse in attendance, encountered a formidable force of 600 soldiers encamped on the north side of the Powder River. The soldiers were chaperoning an engineering party of 20 railroad employees. Spotted Eagle halted his band of warriors, quickly met in council, and tried to decide whether to give up the search for Crow that they had initially undertaken and instead do battle with the soldiers.

By morning the following day, with young, hotheaded warriors having taken matters into their own hands, fighting broke out between the Plains Indians and the U.S. Army. From high on an overlook point, Sitting Bull and Crazy Horse oversaw the battle. The itancan-in-chief then did something that, more than any other deed in his entire life, solidified his status as an imaginative and truly gutsy warrior.

Without hesitation, Sitting Bull calmly fetched his pipe and tobacco pouch, walked from the bluff where he had been standing, and descended into the open valley to within view of the soldiers' line. Seating himself on the ground, Sitting Bull shouted, as quoted by Robert Utley, "Who other Indians wish to smoke with me come."

With White Bull, Gets-the-Best-Of, and two Cheyennes having hesitantly joined their leader, Sitting Bull looked around and calmly smoked, as soldier bullets sang through the air and kicked up dirt but a few feet from the smoking party. When the tobacco had all burned, Sitting Bull, according to Utley, "picked up a stick and thoroughly cleaned the bowl, stowed the pipe in its pouch, rose to his feet, and slowly walked back to the admiring knot of fellow tribesmen." The other smokers chose to run back, with Gets-the-Best-Of leaving his bow and arrows on the ground. White Bull had to return to retrieve the weapons.

The railroad expedition was so shook up with Sitting Bull's display of bravado, the company's engineers refused to go forward, instead hurrying back to the safety of Fort Ellis. The Hunkpapa, with their intimidating tactics, had halted *wasichu* advancement, at least for a while.

PAHA SAPA

The Sioux called them *Paha Sapa*, meaning "Hills that are Black." Occupying 6,000 square miles (15,539 square km) of picturesque mountain country in the western third of the Great Sioux Reservation, the Black Hills rose 4,000 feet (1,220 meters) above the yellow plains surrounding them. Rich in game and wood for tepee poles, the valleys within provided ideal protection for winter camping. To the Sioux, the Black Hills were a "meat pack," a source of sustenance. The Sioux might roam all around the western Plains, but when they were in need of food and shelter, they could go to the Black Hills and partake.

The Sioux looked upon *Paha Sapa* as theirs, never to be given up. The Treaty of 1868 assured Sioux ownership of the Black Hills. No white man had a right to be there. Indeed, into the early 1870s, whites had little reason to venture into the mountainous region, with the area remaining more or less unknown and unexplored by the *wasichu*. Those brave souls who did enter its Indian-defended cavernous hills and valleys rarely succeeded in leaving.

Then came the rumors of gold in the Black Hills. In response, in July 1874, Lieutenant Colonel George Armstrong Custer led a geological survey team out of Fort Abraham Lincoln deep into the heart of Paha Sapa to see if gold did indeed exist there. It did! The rush was on, with thousands of miners rapidly flooding the Black Hills with picks and shovels.

Though obviously in violation of the Fort Laramie Treaty, the miners, nonetheless, kept pouring in—15,000 by 1875. The army was supposed to keep them out but was clearly unable and unwilling to do so. In response to the conflicting situation, the government offered to buy the Black Hills from the Sioux. Red Cloud, now an agency American Indian, was willing to sell—if the price was right. Sitting Bull, of course, was aghast. He cared nothing for the gold that was there. To him, the Black Hills were a food pack, or a place to go when the poor had nothing.

The United States government, pressed to open treaty lands to white miners, yet fearful that its honor would be trashed should

The Black Hills in South Dakota, also known as *Paha Sapa* to the Sioux, was a place for an American Indian family to relocate to when they needed to eat or a place to stay. When gold was discovered in these historic hills, miners rushed to the area, which was a direct violation of the Fort Laramie Treaty of 1868. In an effort to seize the land for themselves, the U.S. government turned its back on the treaty and sent soldiers to combat the American Indians in the area.

it violate treaty promises, took what it felt was the only road open to it—war. Characterizing Sitting Bull and his roving bands as, according to Robert Utley, "wild, hostile, lofty, independent, arrogant, defiant, and contemptuous of government authority," the government decided to send troops against these rebellious Natives to whip them into submission.

In December 1875, the U.S. Army, having taken jurisdiction over hostiles from the Department of the Interior, issued an ultimatum. It sent runners into hostile territory to demand that all Plains

Indians who were out come in or face the wrath of U.S. forces that would arrive to drive them in. Sitting Bull and his people were to cease being hostiles and move themselves onto the eastern portion of the Great Sioux Reservation by January 31, 1876, or else.

It is doubtful that Sitting Bull ever encountered a government runner, traveling in the dead of winter, with the message to give up and head east. Of course, the chief would eventually get the word. No matter. No way was Sitting Bull coming in; no way would he give up the Black Hills and become an agency American Indian like Red Cloud. All-out war between the United States government and the "hostile" Lakota Sioux was now inevitable.

SOLDIERS UPSIDE DOWN

As winter warmed into spring, and spring into the summer of the nation's centennial year of 1876, Sitting Bull and Crazy Horse, along with their determined followers, stayed far from any American Indian reservation. They wanted nothing from the wasichu but to be left alone.

By early June, the tribes had gathered in the Rosebud Valley, 45 miles (72 km) above the Yellowstone and 8 miles (13 km) below the mouth of Muddy Creek, in what is today southern Montana. The Hunkpapa were there, as were their Cheyenne allies. For days, the Sioux would perform their annual Sun Dance. Other tribes, though not participating directly, would gather to watch. For Sitting Bull, a main participant, it would be the most prophetic Sun Dance of his life. For many others, such as White Bull and Wooden Leg, it would be an event to be recalled in cherished detail in the years to come.

At the center of a Sun Dance lodge, a tall log pole rises up, often as high as 20 feet (6 m). A Sioux warrior believes that by suffering at the pole he takes upon himself the agony of his people. He imagines he is offering his body and soul to Wakan Tanka, the Great Spirit. The flesh of the warrior is seen as representing ignorance. Thus a man will pierce his body with skewers hung from the center pole,

The Sioux annually participated in a religious ceremony called the Sun Dance, where warriors would fast and sacrifice their bodies to the Great Spirit. Believing that suffering at the center of the lodge pole was to take on the suffering of their people, the chest or backs of Sioux warriors would be pierced and then attached to these poles. During one of these ceremonies, Sitting Bull had a prophetic vision of an upcoming American Indian victory against the U.S. military.

and if he then dances in such a way as to tear the skewers from his chest and back, he frees himself from darkness. The Sioux warrior's body scars remain with him for life, a reminder to all of his devotion to Wakan Tanka.

After spending a night without food or sleep, Sitting Bull rose the next day to enter the Sun Dance circle. He was naked except for a strip of buckskin around his waist. The chief had blue stripes painted across his shoulders, representing the sky.

Then, according to Albert Marrin, "Sitting Bull sat on the ground with his back to the dance pole, his legs fully extended and his arms resting on his thighs. His adopted brother, Jumping Bull, knelt at his side. Jumping Bull took an awl and a knife from a beaded pouch. Raising the chief's right arm, he stuck the awl into the skin at the base of the wrist. Slowly, carefully, he raised the skin and cut off a piece the size of a pinhead. Then he withdrew the awl and inserted it higher up. He continued this way until he cut 50 pieces of flesh in a straight line ending at the shoulder blade. Jumping Bull then cut another fifty pieces from the left arm."

During the entire half-hour ordeal of bloodletting, Sitting Bull neither flinched nor let out a sound. Silently, he begged Wakan Tanka to have mercy upon his people.

After the sacrificing of his flesh, Sitting Bull rose to dance around the center lodge pole, all the while looking directly into the sun. He danced continuously for a day-and-a-half. Finally, the Hunkpapa chief halted, bent his neck back, and stared wide-eyed into the blazing sun. All those around sensed that Sitting Bull had received a powerful message. Gently laying him to the ground, fellow Hunkpapa brought water to sprinkle over his body.

Black Moon, having knelt to listen to Sitting Bull whisper his vision, rose to convey the chief's message to the multitudes. Sitting Bull had seen soldiers without ears, that is, soldiers refusing to listen, hurtling through the sky. They were upside down, falling like grasshoppers into an Indian village below.

Sitting Bull's vision meant a great battle was imminent. In it, all the soldiers would die, a fact made clear by their inversion. The Sioux would win a great victory.

THE BATTLE OF THE ROSEBUD

On June 15, with the Sun Dance completed, the Sioux packed up their belongings and headed out, arriving two days later at the head of Rosebud Creek. Soon, young warriors from nearby reservations joined the swelling camp, bringing with them rumors of bluecoats marching from three directions. "Three Stars," General George Crook, was advancing from the south. "The One Who Limps" (Colonel John Gibbon) was coming from the west. And "One Star

Terry" (Alfred Terry) and "Long Hair George Armstrong Custer" were marching from the east. Perhaps the mighty battle that Sitting Bull had prophesized was soon to commence?

On the morning of June 17, Crook, with his Crow and Shoshone allies, woke from a fitful night's rest, having camped at the bend of the Rosebud. Within moments, the general found himself engaged in what would be the biggest cavalry fight in North America since the Civil War.

Crazy Horse, who would lead the contest for the Sioux, had, upon arriving on the scene, just completed a 50-mile (80-km) ride in the dark. Demonstrating tactical brilliance, he attacked Crook headlong, using a more concentrated force than few American Indian leaders ever employed in battle. Crazy Horse ordered his warriors to charge straight into the soldiers and break their lines, "white man" style.

For six hours the battle raged on, with each side charging and countercharging. Fearing torture should they be captured, soldiers passed the word, "No surrender." John F. Finerty, a reporter with Crook's forces, wrote in his notebook, as quoted by Albert Marrin, "Each one of us would have blown out his own brains rather than fall alive into Indian hands."

Sitting Bull, while active in exhorting his men to fight, crying out, "Steady men, remember how to hold a gun," did not directly participate. His arms were swollen and all but useless from the flesh-giving of the Sun Dance a few days earlier.

When the battle was over, Crazy Horse, having lost a dozen men, withdrew. Based on a United States military doctrine that noted whoever held the originally contested ground was the winner, Crook claimed victory. Yet the general's forces were badly mauled. He took his men south again, where he would lick his wounds, and, significantly, withdraw from any future engagements in the three-prong campaign that aimed to annihilate the Sioux.

Although the Battle of the Rosebud did not see "soldiers falling into camp," as Sitting Bull had envisioned during his Sun Dance, the war with the wasichu was by no means over. "One Star Terry," with golden-hair, buckskin resplendent George Armstrong Custer, was advancing from the east. Sitting Bull's Sun Dance vision was yet a possibility.

BOUND FOR GLORY

"In appearance, manner, and garb, he cut a distinctive figure," Robert Utley wrote of Custer in his classic treatment *Custer: Cavalier in Buckskin*. "Reddish-gold hair fell in curls almost to his shoulders. A brushy mustache hid a dimpled, receding chin. His fair complexion burned easily in the sun, giving his high cheeks and aquiline nose a perpetually flushed aspect and setting off bright blue eyes. The quick, jerky movement of his sinewy frame, together with speech rushing forth in high-pitched bursts bordering on a stutter, betrayed an unceasing and hyperkinetic restlessness."

That restlessness cut both ways for Custer, a West Point graduate. Having been labeled "The Boy General" for his promotion to the rank at the age of 25 during the Civil War, making him the youngest major general in the Union Army at the time, Custer was a true hero. Yet in the decade following the Civil War, the man's vanity, pettiness, and cruelty were quick to surface. Out West, where Custer was sent to fight American Indians, he was often seen as a brutal tyrant of the worst order. "Custer ordered poor troopers to have half their heads shaved as a mark of disgrace or ordered them flogged," Louis S. Warren reported in *Buffalo Bill's America*. "He threw them into the deep circular pit he used as a guard-house in Hays, for offenses as minor as leaving camp for forty-five minutes to buy a tin of fruit (which soldiers frequently did to fend off rampant scurvy)."

For instances like these, and for more serious offenses, such as abandoning soldiers in the field, Custer was court-martialed in 1867. Nonetheless, restored to service the following year, Custer saw his stature rise when he accompanied General Philip Sheridan in an attack on Cheyenne Chief Black Kettle's village on the Washita River. It would be the army's biggest victory of the Plains' campaigns to that point. Custer, it would seem, was bound for glory.

A decade later, when Custer joined One Star Terry in the summer of 1876 as part of a campaign to hunt and destroy hostile

General George Armstrong Custer (*seated, surrounded by his scouts*) gained a reputation during the Civil War for being fearless and aggressive. Despite being court-martialed twice in his military career, Custer was asked back to help in several military campaigns against American Indians. He famously underestimated American Indian warriors and led his men into the Battle of Little Bighorn, an ambush that is commonly known as "Custer's Last Stand."

American Indians in and around the Bighorn Mountains, his prowess as an American Indian fighter had solidified. Though a polarizing figure still, Custer, like Terry, was out to destroy, to wipe out, any and all American Indians he could find.

Buffalo Extermination

The demise of the buffalo, or American bison, began in the 1860s when buffalo hunters took aim at the noble creatures in order to fill the bellies of railroad workers and settlers expanding across the Plains. Then sportsmen got into the act, slaughtering buffalo for the mere fun of it. In the early 1870s, with the discovery of new tanning methods, the kill rate went up exponentially. There are those, however, who believe that an "unofficial" policy of extermination, promoted by the U.S. government, was what really did the buffalo in. If the buffalo were decimated, American Indians would have no choice but to give up their hunting ways, "come in," and take up residency on reservations, where they would be taught to be herders and farmers. No one more forcefully expressed this view than General Philip Sheridan. In a famous statement, written in 1875, the general declared, as reported in *Buffalo Bill and Sitting Bull: Inventing the Wild West*:

> Buffalo hunters have done in the past two years and will do more in the next year to settle the vexed Indian question, than the entire regular army has done in the past thirty years. They are destroying the Indians' commissary, and it is a well-known fact that any army losing its base of supplies is placed at a great disadvantage. Send them powder and lead, if you will; for the sake of a lasting peace, let them kill, skin and sell until the buffaloes are exterminated. Then your prairies can be covered with speckled cattle and the festive cowboy, who follows the hunter as a second forerunner of an advanced civilization.

After several weeks of marching in the late spring, Terry and Custer, coming from the east, reached the Yellowstone River in Montana Territory in late June. On June 22, Terry sent Custer and the Seventh Cavalry to the mouth of the Rosebud with orders to proceed upstream with the hope of finding an Indian trail. From there, Custer was to advance still farther until he entered the Little Bighorn Valley from the south.

Lieutenant Colonel Custer (his rank having been reduced after the Civil War) did as he was ordered, and on June 24 his scouts announced that they had found signs of American Indians. The Indian trail led west into the valley of the Little Bighorn River. On the morning of June 25, Custer's troops climbed a high ridge south of Ash Creek known as Crow's Nest. Then, according to Joseph M. Marshall III, "As the daylight brightened, through a field glass they were able to discern movement in the floodplain west of the Little Bighorn River. The scouts knew that the movement in the distance could only be a very large herd of horses." Indeed, on the horizon, like "maggots in the grass," were 12,000 to 15,000 horses, supporting the largest concentration of Plains Indians ever to assemble. The mother of all Indian war battles was soon to begin.

MISCALCULATION

Estimates are that upward of 10,000 American Indians, 1,800 of them seasoned, well-armed, and well-led warriors, were now gathered at what they called the Greasy Grass, but what whites would forever identify as the Little Bighorn. Their camp consisted of five tribal circles of Sioux and one of Cheyenne. Sitting Bull, Crazy Horse, and Gaul were there, as were many other tribal leaders. Children, parents, and grandparents filled the 1,000 lodges that stretched for more than 2 miles (3.2 km) along the Bighorn River and 200 yards (182 m) abreast at the widest point. Troops advancing on the American Indian encampment numbered less than 600.

Sustaining a campsite of this size severely drained local resources. At 25 pounds (11 kilograms) of dried meat per household, this group would consume 12.5 tons (11.3 metric tons). From 10,000 to 15,000 pounds (4,535 to 6,803 kg) of dried fruits and vegetables would be eaten. And, at 20 pounds (9 kg) of forage per day, the herd of 15,000 horses was capable of downing 100 to 150 tons (90 to 136 metric tons) of hay. Clearly, such a large gathering of American Indians could not stay together in one place for long; the local ecosystem would collapse. When George Armstrong Custer arrived on the scene, he had every reason to believe that his adversaries were ready to break camp at any moment. As a man bound for glory, he was not about to let that happen. Custer would need to strike at once.

The plan was simple, at least on paper. The lieutenant colonel's command would divide into three attack columns. Custer would lead the eastern column, placed high on a ridge, to hit from the north. Major Marcus Reno would charge from the south. And Captain Frederick Benteen would go wide on the west to cut off any American Indians who, as Bill Yenne declared, "tried to escape the hammer and anvil of Custer."

By 2 P.M. on June 25, the battle was on, with Reno's three companies attacking first, crashing into the south end of the huge American Indian encampment, right into Sitting Bull's band of Hunkpapa. "I was lying in my lodge," the chief told an interviewer in October of the following year, as reported by Bill Yenne. "Some young men ran in to me and said: 'the Long Hair is in the camp. Get up. They are firing into the camp.' I said all right. I jumped up and stepped out of my lodge."

Custer was not actually in the camp, however, but on a ridge farther north. It was Reno that Sitting Bull and his Hunkpapa were facing, and in the ensuing fight the major and his forces were completely routed, pinned down so that those who survived could in no way aid Custer and his contingent ready to attack from the north.

Accounts vary as to Sitting Bull's role in fending off Reno's charge. Some say he stood in camp, firing at advancing troops. Others claim he did not fight at all that day, but, nonetheless, shouted encouragement to younger warriors. Either way, upon Reno's defeat, Sitting Bull mounted up and rode north through the village. He was sure that the assault he had just witnessed would not be the only one coming from the wasichu soldiers that day.

LIKE GRASSHOPPERS FALLING

With Reno's squadron of 175 soldiers having been all but killed, and with Benteen far back on the trail somewhere, it was left to Custer, with his 210 men, to take the fight to the Hunkpapa. Yet having fragmented the 7th Regiment, the lieutenant colonel was in a desperate situation. After earlier attempts at offense, he was soon forced to fall back atop a knob of high ground, which is today known as Custer Hill, or Last Stand Hill.

Charging to reach that hill, hoping to surround and defeat Custer, were bands of Cheyenne, Hunkpapa, and Oglala warriors. Lame White Man and Gaul led the charge for the Cheyenne and Hunkpapa, respectively, crossing the Bighorn River, crashing into Custer's few remaining rearguard bluecoats, and forcing them up the ridge to Last Stand Hill. Crazy Horse, with a large band of Oglala, headed downstream and doubled back in a sweeping arc from the north. "The giant pincer's movement engulfed Custer's little squadron," the authors of *Indian Wars* reported, "and Indians poured in upon him from all directions."

By all accounts, Custer and his men fought bravely. Yet in less than an hour, every one of them lay dead. "The trouble with the soldiers," Sitting Bull, who was not actually engaged in the fight, told interviewers later, as reported by Bill Yenne, "was that they were so exhausted and their horses bothered them so much that they could not take good aim. Some of their horses broke away from them and left them to stand and drop and die."

There are those who claim that Custer was the last man standing and that he went down with guns in both hands blazing. The story, however, is a myth, concocted no doubt to attach heroic stature to the 7th Cavalry leader. It has also been said that Custer's body was mutilated. Though the bodies of his fellow soldiers were, indeed, butchered (in many cases by outraged American Indian women and children), Custer's body was not. "My people did not want his scalp," Sitting Bull was to have declared. "I have said, he was a great chief."

Gravely misjudging the abilities of the American Indians, General George Armstrong Custer led his men in an attack against an American Indian camp. The camp included the Sioux and Cheyenne and some of those tribes' fiercest warriors and most important leaders, including Sitting Bull. Custer and his men died in the Battle of Little Bighorn, a conflict that is remembered as one of the worst military defeats in U.S. history.

Custer's defeat was an extraordinary victory for the Lakota and their allies. In turn, Little Bighorn was one of the most complete disasters in American military annals. When Custer's troops had tried to attack the American Indian village, and they came tumbling down headfirst into camp, like grasshoppers falling, it seemed Sitting Bull's Sun Dance vision had been realized. Yet part of that vision also told of a curse that would befall all Lakota should they steal, as they did, from the white soldiers at the Greasy Grass. The Sioux would forever become addicted to *wasichu* things, the prophecy declared. Despite their incredible victory, the Lakota had every reason to fear what the future might bring them.

WINTER OF DISCONTENT

Vengeance! Retribution! Punishment! Upon the death of Custer and his men, a grieving and angry nation demanded reprisal.

Whites, calling what happened at Little Bighorn a massacre, went crazy with indignation. "Custer Avengers" flocked to Sioux lands, eager to engage in any military action. "Hostiles," above all, were to be punished, driven deep onto reservations; to be treated as prisoners of war. If such hunting bands insisted on staying out, they would be annihilated. There would be no more talk of peace; the army would take complete control of American Indian affairs. George "Three Stars" Crook, Alfred Terry, and other military commanders were out to punish the American Indians for humiliating the U.S. Army.

Less than two months after the June 25 debacle at Little Bighorn, the government's Great Council, in blatant violation of the 1868 treaty, took the Powder River country and the Black Hills away from the American Indians. "The 'unceded lands' in the Powder were being unilaterally 'ceded,' and the Black Hills were legally open to wasichu settlement," Bill Yenne reported. "The tide of wasichu that had seemed to be ebbing eight winters earlier was running like a tidal wave."

Sitting Bull and his followers, having celebrated their Big-horn victory and mourned their dead, broke camp on June 26 and headed out, hoping to find wandering herds of the ever-diminishing buffalo. Yet as the days and weeks progressed, bands separated and went their own way. Disagreements among the Sitting Bull-led Sioux was increasing. Some, such as American Horse and his supporters, simply preferred to return to the reservation, at least to spend the winter.

On September 9, near Slim Buttes, Captain Anson Mills, serving under George Crook, fell upon American Horse and his entourage. Women and children were maimed and slain. American Horse, buckshot having torn his entrails out, would soon die from the encounter.

Sitting Bull, upon hearing of the Slim Buttes battle, rushed to the scene with about 600 warriors but arrived too late to provide help. "What have we done that the white people want us to stop," Sitting Bull declared, as reported in *Bury My Heart at Wounded Knee*. "We have been running up and down this country, but they follow us from one place to another."

Indeed, attacks by the wasichu on "fugitive" American Indians would only increase in the months to come, even as, most ominously, winter approached.

PARLEY

Sitting Bull did not go looking for trouble. He did not hate the white man; he did not wish to fight him. The Lakota chief wanted above all to be left alone, to hunt on fertile land as his father and his father's father had done. Though Sitting Bull was willing to trade with the wasichu, he did not want his people to become dependent on the goods such trade would bring. Sitting Bull did not need a vision to tell him that such dependence would be a noose that would lead his people to destruction.

Yet the white man was here, and it was clear he wasn't just passing through. He not only had come to stay, he had also come to compel hostiles, such as Sitting Bull, to surrender and come in, to become wards of the state.

On October 15, Sitting Bull's band of Hunkpapas, Miniconjous, and Sans Arcs intersected a train of 86 wagons, accompanied by a guard of 200 soldiers, many armed with long-range infantry rifles. A fight ensued, in which White Bull, Sitting Bull's nephew, was shot in the arm. The next day, in an attempt to convey his feelings about the wasichu presence in his land, Sitting Bull sought to communicate with the army accompanying the wagon train. He summoned an intermediary and had him write a message for the wasichu. Impaled on a stick, then thrust into the middle of the road in front of the wagon train, his extraordinary letter read, as quoted in *The Lance and the Shield*:

> I want to know what you are doing traveling on this road. You scare all the buffalo away. I want to hunt on the place. I want you to turn back from here. If you don't, I will fight you again. I want you to leave what you have got here, and turn back from here.
> I am your friend,
> > SITTING BULL
>
> I mean all the rations you have got and some powder. I wish you would write as soon as you can.

Clumsy as the letter was, Sitting Bull had made clear where he stood. To the chief it was simple. The Yellowstone was his country. The soldiers were invaders. The wasichu scared the buffalo away. If the soldiers did not leave, he would fight them—to the death.

Of course, Lieutenant Colonel Elwell S. Otis, head of the army command, and to whom the letter was addressed, was not going to withdraw. The wagon train was left to resume its progress, while the Indians rode off.

Vision Quest

When a young Sioux boy was 12 or 13, he went on a vision quest, lasting from one to four days, during which he was required to fast in a quiet, lonely place. In doing so, it was expected the boy would receive a vision that would tell his future. The vision, if it came, would appear as a sign from a guiding spirit. That spirit would usually take the form of an animal. When the boy returned to camp, he was taken to a shaman, or medicine man, who would help him interpret his vision.

Before going on a vision quest, however, a young man would need to endure the trials of a sweat lodge. Such a lodge was usually a dome-shaped tent made of willow branches covered with hides and blankets. In the center of the lodge was a pit.

The idea behind the sweat lodge was to achieve a physical and spiritual purification before undertaking the vision quest. The *Plains Indian* Web site offers details on the sweat lodge ceremony:

A leader (the teacher) and a fire keeper (responsible for the fire, wood, stones, water, and other supplies) took part in the ceremony along with other participants. The fire keeper brought heated stones into the lodge and the leader placed the stones in the pit. When the fire keeper closed the door to the lodge the inside heated up. Water was poured over the stones. The inside became very hot and steamy. There was praying, singing and drumming as well as the burning of sweet grass and smoking a pipe. The sweet grass, pipes, and prayers were offerings to the spirits. At the end of the ceremony the participants would go outside and lay on the grass to cool off.

STRESSED OUT

Sitting Bull talked a tough game, demanding that the wasichu abandon "his" country, that his fellow tribesman forgo the white man's seductive annuities, and that the chief simply be allowed to follow the traditional hunting path laid out by his forefathers. In truth, however, as fall turned to winter, Sitting Bull began to become distressed. The soldiers, he knew, were not going to give up in their attempt to get their way—complete surrender. And the chief saw that, all around him, his coalition was unraveling. "The defection of the Sans Arc and Miniconjou chiefs disclosed that not all the hunting bands possessed his [Sitting Bull's] stubborn aversion to giving up their freedom and living at the agencies," Robert Utley noted. "Even his nephew White Bull had gone with them. Sitting Bull was increasingly isolated."

Then there was the appearance of Colonel Nelson Miles, referred to by the Sioux as the "Man-with-the Bear Coat," or simply "Bear Coat." Every bit the egotist that Custer ever was, Bear Coat hungered obsessively for power, promotion, and distinction. And, most ominously for the hostiles, Bear Coat was willing, even eager, to pursue them in the dead of winter, all the better to find his adversaries at their most vulnerable.

A hastily convened meeting with Bear Coat, on October 20, did not go well for Sitting Bull. Irreconcilable positions soon became apparent. Their parley, or conference, at Cedar Creek led nowhere.

The Sioux chief's failure to gain any concessions, short of surrender, from Colonel Miles was due, in part, to the commander's keen sense of where his enemy stood, where his strengths and weaknesses appeared. As Miles wrote to his wife after the meeting with Sitting Bull, as reported in *The Lance and the Shield*:

> The man is apparently forty-five or fifty-years-old. He has a large broad head and strong features. He is a man evidently of great influence and a thinking, reasoning being. I should judge his great strength is as a warrior. I think he feels that his strength is somewhat exhausted and he appeared much depressed, suffering from nervous excitement and loss of power. . . . At times he was almost inclined to accept the situation, but I think partly from fear and partly through the belief that he might do

Determined still to preserve Sioux land, Sitting Bull (*left*) met with Colonel Nelson A. Miles (*right*) in the hopes of negotiating an agreement that would satisfy both the Sioux and the U.S. government. Nelson, however, knew Sitting Bull was quickly losing support from the members of his tribe and, with winter fast approaching, would soon be vulnerable to attack.

better, he did not accept. I think that many of his people were desirous to make peace.

Clearly, Sitting Bull's situation, his ability to maintain a hunting and warrior life for himself and what was left of his followers, was rapidly deteriorating. And winter was fast approaching.

BANDS ON THE RUN

While Sitting Bull and Bear Coat evaded and dodged each other north of the Yellowstone River, Three Stars Crook set out from Fort

Fetterman, heading north for the Powder River country. It was late November 1876, deep snow drifts lay on the ground, and the temperature often fell to -30°F (-34°C).

The cruel environment noted, General Crook traveled well equipped. With more than 1,100 cavalrymen, plus an army of infantry, his troops (and Pawnee mercenaries) numbered more than 2,000. Crook had enough rations to fill 168 wagons. There was sufficient ammunition and powder to weigh down 400 pack mules. He had plenty of artillery. Three Stars was on a mission to maul, crush, and destroy any and all American Indians he could find.

Though Crook's soldiers were, in particular, looking for Crazy Horse, on the morning of November 25 his command stumbled upon Dull Knife's Cheyenne village. The Cheyenne had slipped away from the Red Cloud agency, searching for food after the authorities there had halted their rations. Crook immediately sent Three Fingers, also known as Colonel Ranald S. Mackenzie, against this village of 150 lodges.

The result was devastation. "They caught the Cheyennes in their lodges, killing many of them as they came awake," Dee Brown reported. "Others ran out naked into the biting cold, the warriors trying to fight off the Pawnees and the onrushing soldiers long enough for their women and children to escape."

The Cheyenne lost almost everything: meat, tepees, clothing, and ammunition as they tried to rise up and flee their tormentors. During the first night of flight, 12 babies froze to death in their mothers' arms. Then, according to Dee Brown, "The next night, the men killed some of the ponies, disemboweled them, and thrust small children inside to keep them from freezing to death. The old people put their hands and feet in beside the children."

The Cheyenne sought, and eventually found, Crazy Horse's camp on the upper Tongue River. The Oglala chief fed and sheltered his charges the best he could. But Crazy Horse warned the Cheyenne that with Bear Coat looking for them in the north, and Three Stars coming up from the south, they would all have to keep moving, keep running.

As one of the bravest warriors and most important leaders of the Sioux, Crazy Horse remained undefeated in battle against the U.S. Army. During the winter of 1876-1877, however, Crazy Horse was forced to constantly move his people to avoid being attacked by U.S. forces. Cold, tired, and hungry, the American Indian leader had no choice but to surrender.

DISARMED AND DISMOUNTED

Onward Crazy Horse ran, pursued at all times by wasichu soldiers.

On January 15, 1877, the Oglala chief met up with Sitting Bull at the mouth of Prairie Dog Creek, where the Tongue River bursts forth from the Bighorn Mountains, in what was then Montana Territory. Most of the other hunting bands (hostiles) were there. Black Moccasin and Ice (White Bull) of the Cheyenne were in camp. Black Shield and Lame Deer of the Miniconjous were present, as were Spotted Eagle and Red Bear of the Sans Arcs. Sitting Bull probably commanded no more than 15 to 20 lodges at this time, down, devastatingly, from the hundreds he controlled in the summer of 1876.

Dissension filled the frigid air.

The Miniconjous and the Sans Arcs wanted to surrender. The Hunkpapa, Oglala, and the Cheyenne argued for continued resistance. Unable to unite for a single purpose, the tribes split up. Sitting Bull turned north out of the Powder River country. Crazy Horse went south.

In late April, Red Cloud, in residence at his own agency, was asked to seek out Crazy Horse and offer him what the wasichu considered generous surrender terms. "The people who traveled with Crazy Horse were hungry, and they were running short of ammunition with which to hunt and to continue the armed struggle against the U.S. Army," Bill Yenne reported. "Red Cloud counseled the younger man [Crazy Horse] to come in."

On May 6, 1877, Crazy Horse, along with 889 Indians, 12,000 ponies, and 117 arms went to Camp Robinson, Nebraska, and surrendered. As Dee Brown noted, "The last of the Sioux war chiefs now became a reservation Indian, disarmed, dismounted, with no authority over his people, a prisoner of the Army, which had never defeated him in battle."

At the same time that Crazy Horse was going in, Sitting Bull and his small band of loyal followers were rushing northward. If he would not give up, and if he could not continue the fight with the U. S. government, he would go where he felt his people might find peace. On or around May 7, 1877, Sitting Bull crossed the *chanku wakan*, the sacred road, into the Grandmother's Country, the land of the Red Coats—the British Dominion of Canada.

GRANDMOTHER'S REFUGE

Canada's Northwest Territory, the vast, relatively underpopulated land west of Ontario, was a wild and lawless place in the years before Sitting Bull crossed over the border. When Canada took over control of the region from the Hudson's Bay Company in 1869, strife was rampant. Whiskey traders abounded, setting up stations such as Fort Whoop-up, Spitzee, and Robbers' Roost. "They encouraged tribesmen to exchange furs for 'white lightning,'" Albert Marrin reported. "As a result, hundreds died each year in drunken brawls. Warriors, driven crazy by whiskey, sometimes murdered their own families."

The Canadian government had neither the means nor the will to send an army into the Northwest Territory to establish law and order, or to suppress "their" Native Peoples. Instead, in 1873, the government, under the leadership of its first prime minister, Sir John Macdonald, established a special type of police force, to be known as the Northwest Mounted Police, or Mounties. Dressed in red, like British redcoats, the Mounties, a mere 300 of them, soon fanned out in an attempt to tame the Canadian wild frontier.

It seemed an impossible task. How could so few Mounties achieve their objective in bringing stability to such an endless region? In part, the Mounties succeeded with the use of fear, or, actually, the lack of it. Above all, a Mountie was admonished never to show apprehension when in the presence of adversaries, no matter how many or how well-armed. He was always to ride tall in the saddle, literally and figuratively. Furthermore, Mounties were told they could go anywhere, anytime, and that this land was theirs to patrol and protect—all of it. The Mounties were the law. Indeed, as Marrin observed, "They were more than a police force; they were a complete legal system on horseback. Not only did they close the whiskey forts and arrest lawbreakers, they acted as judges, passing sentences and exacting punishment. Above all, they kept their word."

Mounties, too, benefited from a reputation for fair play. Everyone, be he white, black, or Canadian Indian, was to be treated equally before Canadian law. Furthermore, the Canadians knew that the way the Americans had been dealing with their Native Peoples was appalling. If American Indians were making trouble south of the border, many whites in Canada felt that the U.S. government had only itself to blame.

Thus, for many reasons, Sitting Bull and his fleeing tribe were justified in heading north, in escaping the hands of grasping bluecoats who sought to destroy or enslave them.

THE QUEEN'S REPRESENTATIVE

Within a day of his crossing, Sitting Bull came face to face with a new type of wasichu, in the person of 34-year-old Major James M. Walsh, known for being a "Mountie's Mountie."

Walsh, by all accounts, was a stubborn, domineering man. Commander of Fort Walsh, the Northwest Mounted Police inspector was known to cuss a blue streak whenever his impatience got the best of him, which was often. Yet Walsh exemplified, perhaps better than any Mountie ever did, the qualities of fairness, firmness, courage, tolerance, justice, honesty, and kindness that his police force was to become famous for. Canadian Indians knew Walsh as "White Forehead." The Sioux gave him the name *Wahonkeza*, but also called

Desperate for peace and a place where his people could rest, Sitting Bull fled to Canada with his remaining supporters. Shortly after their arrival, a group of Canadian Mounties met Sitting Bull to establish the terms of the Sioux's stay in Canada. Although the Sioux would not have their own lands or receive annuities, Sitting Bull was satisfied with the agreement he made with the Canadians.

him "Long Lance," after they first noticed the red-and-white pennants the Mounties carried on parade.

On May 7, 1877, Walsh, a sergeant, and three troopers set out to investigate rumors of Sitting Bull's presence in the drab hills and ravines of Pinto Horse Butte. Around noon, the five Canadians spotted Native Peoples sitting motionless on hilltops, watching them. As Walsh and his men rode on, straight as a lance in the saddle, more Native Peoples appeared, eventually surrounding the small, red-coated police force. The Native Peoples, strangely, made no attempt to stop Walsh. Moments later, the major and his men came upon a large camp. According to *Sitting Bull and the Mounties*, "Reining in, they sat in their saddles while a group of Indians rode toward them. Spotted Eagle, war chief of the Sans Arc Sioux, told them they were the first white men to dare approach Sitting Bull's camp so unconcernedly."

Shortly, Sitting Bull himself approached, accompanied by a group of lesser chiefs. The Lakota chief and the Canadian Mountie eyed each other. In Walsh, Sitting Bull observed a man who was as wiry as a mountain lion. In Sitting Bull, Walsh saw a leader who had a muscular build yet was bowlegged and walked with a limp. The two shook hands. In time, they would become lifelong trusted friends.

When Walsh asked Sitting Bull why he had come to Queen Victoria's country, the reply was simple. "We seek sanctuary," the chief declared. His people were desperate for peace, for a place to protect their women and children. "Yesterday I was fleeing from white men, cursing them as I went," Sitting Bull offered, as reported in *The North-West Mounted Police 1873–1893*. "Today they erect their lodges by the side of mine and defy me. The White Forehead Chief (Walsh) walks to my lodge alone and unarmed. He gives me the hand of peace. Have I fallen? Am I at the end?"

SITTING BULL'S NEW BOSS

All this was well and good, the fact that Sitting Bull had found a new home where he and his people might resume their hunting ways, free from wasichu harassment. But "not so fast" was a message Walsh wished to convey as quickly as possible. As the major sat with Sitting Bull in conference that fateful day, the Mountie made clear to the chief that there would be some "dos and don'ts," laws and rules, he would be expected to abide by if the Sioux wished to stay in the Grandmother's Country. Sitting Bull, his immediate followers, and the Sioux who had arrived before him would have to behave themselves.

The White Mother's laws, Walsh was quick to point out, applied to everyone—white, black, and red. Yet those same laws punished everyone equally, should they be violated. The Sioux must not war against other tribes. They must not steal horses or anything else. They must not kill or injure anyone. And, above all, Sitting Bull must make sure that none of his people used the Grandmother's Country as refuge from which to launch raids across the border at American settlements or soldiers. If they did that, asylum in Canada would be forfeited.

Furthermore, Walsh went on to intimate, the Sioux could not expect any Canadian government handouts, or annuities. They would not be fed by the government; they would need to hunt for their own food and trade for supplies. And, Sitting Bull was not to expect that the Canadian government would ever provide them with a reservation, a land exclusive for their own use.

Sitting Bull was evidently pleased with what Walsh had told him, at least at the time. The chief showed the Mountie a group of medals King George III had given his grandfather in gratitude for the man's service to the British Crown during the War of 1812. Sitting Bull's grandfather had supposedly told the future Lakota chief, as quoted in *Sitting Bull and the Mounties*, "If you should ever wish to find peace, go north to the land of the redcoats."

It did not take long for Sitting Bull to witness Walsh's firm hand in support of the queen's justice. On May 8, as the police prepared to leave the Sioux camp, White Dog and two other Assiniboines appeared herding five stolen horses. Walsh stepped over to White Dog and placed him under arrest. "Tell me where you got these horses, how you got them, and what you intend doing with them, or I'll clamp these irons on you and take you away," the major was to have said, as quoted in *Sitting Bull and the Mounties*. White Dog, expecting aid from the throng of Sioux warriors who had gathered to watch the unfolding drama, blustered with defiance. When it was apparent that Walsh was not going to back down, however, White Dog mumbled something about finding the horses on the prairie.

The Tepee—Home on the Plains

The Lakota maintained some of the finest, most practical tepees of all, the home for all Plains Indians. It was the woman's job to take care of the tepee, to set it up and pull it down. The women of a tribe were generally considered the owners of the tepees.

In some cases, a tepee could be set up in less than an hour. According to the *Plains Indian* Web site, here is how it was done:

- Three or four long poles (made from pine trees) formed the basic frame.
- Once these poles were set firmly in the ground, other poles were placed against the frame in the form of a circle.
- The poles leaned together at the top and were fastened with narrow strips of hides to form a cone shape.
- The poles were covered with bison hides and an opening (smoke hole) was left at the top.
- Two longer poles were attached to the smoke-flaps at the top of the tepee.
- The flaps were like a chimney which could be opened to allow the smoke to escape.
- In hot weather the covering was rolled up from the bottom so that air could circulate.
- Wooden pegs were pounded into the ground around the bottom of the tepee covering.
- The opening (door) always faced east, and the tepee was tilted toward the east. A flap covered the opening.
- Depending on the size, it took 8 to 20 hides sewn together with sinew to make the tepee cover.

Walsh prudently chose to accept the explanation and dismissed the thief. White Dog slid away in humiliation, while the Sioux stood dumbfounded by the Mountie's demonstrated courage.

TOO MANY INDIANS

True, if he obeyed the rules, stayed out of trouble, stuck to hunting but not warring, Sitting Bull would avoid being harassed by *wasichu* north of the medicine line (border). Yet that did not mean he and his people had arrived in the Promised Land—far from it. For one thing, the Sioux were not the only American Indians in the Grandmother's Country. Numerous tribes who were native to Canada, roamed and hunted in what is today the provinces of Alberta, Saskatchewan, and Manitoba. Many resented the presence of the Sioux newcomers from south of the border. Resources, such as game, timber, and, particularly, buffalo, were not unlimited. The more hunters who searched the northern Plains, the fewer buffalo there would be. By the late 1870s, the buffalo's diminishing presence had, indeed, become a serious, life-threatening problem.

While the buffalo was always used to its fullest extent by the American Indians, the white man early on discovered the value of particular parts, such as buffalo robes and tongues. In the East, a fine robe made of buffalo hide could bring $50. Sliced tongues were considered a delicacy in New York and Boston. By the 1850s, 100,000 buffalo tongues and hides were being taken every year.

Twenty years later, however, the number of buffalo being slaughtered in the United States had stretched into the millions. Initially, the increase could be explained by the arrival of the American sportsman. One man eager to lead hunting expeditions on to what was often referred to as the "American Serengeti," was none other than Buffalo Bill Cody. Though killing buffalo may not have been what earned him his nickname (selling buffalo meat is what probably did), a popular jingle of the time, as quoted in *Sitting Bull*, glorified his exploits:

> *Buffalo Bill, Buffalo Bill,*
> *Never missed and never will;*
> *Always aims and shoots to kill,*
> *And the company pays his buffalo bill.*

Sitting Bull did not think that the butchering of buffalo, particularly after it reached epidemic proportions with the discovery of how to tan their hides, was a laughing matter. In October 1877, the Lakota chief told an American interviewer, as quoted by Bill Yenne:

> It is strange that Americans should complain that the Indians kill buffaloes. We kill buffaloes, as we kill other animals, for food and clothing, and to make our lodges warm. . . . Your young men shoot for pleasure. All they take from dead buffalo is his tail, or his head, or his horns, perhaps, to show they have killed a buffalo. What is this? Is it robbery? You call us savages. What are they? The buffaloes have come north. We have come north to find them.

But there was a problem. The Canadian buffalo, now being relentlessly hunted by northern American Indians for sustenance, were dying at an alarming rate. For Sitting Bull and his people, tension mounted as the months passed in Grandmother's Country.

SURRENDER

On February 11, 1878, while on a visit to Chicago, Major Walsh was interviewed by a *New York Times* reporter. "To what do you ascribe the rumor that a body of Sioux were seen south of the line?" he was asked. "Some time in November a party of the young bucks while running the buffalo got across the line, and a party of [C]rows killed two of the party and wounded another," Walsh replied. "They were a party of the Yanktonnais Sioux, who are Agency Indians, and who are supposed to belong to the agencies on the Missouri River. . . . Our Sioux [Canadian] did not fight them."

Perhaps Walsh was being kind, trying to protect Sitting Bull and his band of lodges. There is little doubt, however, that Walsh knew only too well that bands of young warrior Sioux were crossing into the United States, if not to raid, at least to find buffalo to slaughter. In the months and years to come, such raids, seen as a matter of life

With nowhere left to turn, Sitting Bull left Canada with his people and headed towards North Dakota Territory, where he would finally surrender at Fort Buford. Instructing his son Crow Foot (*above*) to hand over his rifle to the head military officer of the fort, Sitting Bull was one of the last great Sioux chiefs to give up the battle against the U.S. government.

or death by the Sioux, would increase, causing considerable embarrassment to the Canadian government. By 1880, the queen's representatives had made it clear to Sitting Bull that he was no longer welcome in the Grandmother's Country.

In response, Sitting Bull grew sullen and argumentative. He complained of the Canadian government's lack of compassion for his people. In one instance, the chief all but threatened Walsh, his friend, if he did not provide the Sioux with provisions. The Mountie's reaction was swift and cutting. "Who do you think you are?" he yelled at Sitting Bull, as quoted in *Sitting Bull and the Mounties*. "Have you forgotten that you're American Indians? You haven't any right to be in Canada. You've caused us police any amount of trouble. You've stolen horses. . . . If you keep on making trouble, I'll put the whole d--- lot of you in jail!"

From then on, though Sitting Bull and Major Walsh were able to reconcile, it was downhill for Sitting Bull and the few Plains Indians who had not already deserted him and fled south to reservations in the United States. Finally, on July 19, 1881, Sitting Bull, in response to a full pardon guarantee from the Americans and the near starvation of his tribe, took his family and 150 loyal followers, and crossed over to surrender at Fort Buford (North Dakota Territory).

On July 20, Sitting Bull and his entourage assembled for surrender "ceremonies." Sitting Bull asked his five-year-old son, Crow Foot, to hand his father's rifle to the military commander. Then the chief spoke, as quoted in *The Lance and the Shield*:

> I surrender this rifle to you through my young son, whom I now desire to teach in this manner that he has become a friend of the Americans. I wish him to learn the habits of the whites and to be educated as their sons are educated. I wish to be remembered that I was the last man of my tribe to surrender my rifle. This boy has given it to you, and he now wants to know how he is going to make a living.

9

CELEBRITY PRISONER

Sitting Bull fully expected the United States government to hang him as soon as he crossed the "medicine line," back into the country of his birth. That the authorities did not do so meant that the Hunkpapa chief had become too famous to kill. He had become a celebrity because people mistakenly believed that he was the mastermind of Custer's destruction. "With Sitting Bull's name alongside General Custer's in all the banners, the Battle of Little Bighorn had created headlines all over the world," Bobby Bridger, author of *Buffalo Bill and Sitting Bull*, declared. "The United States would have to answer too many legal questions in the international community if it assassinated Sitting Bull."

Upon realizing that he was not to be done away with, Sitting Bull was quick to request—indeed, demand—that his life (and those of his compatriots) remain more or less as it had been. "I now wish to be allowed to live this side of the line or the other, as I see fit," the chief told an assembled group of wasichu on the day of his surrender, as reported in *New Perspectives on the West*. "I wish to continue my old life of hunting, but would like to be allowed to trade on both sides of the line."

Sitting Bull's appeal was denied. Sadly, the Hunkpapa warrior and hunter had yet to grasp a simple fact—he was no longer in control of his own destiny.

From Fort Buford, Sitting Bull and his supporters were taken down the Missouri River on a steamboat, the *General Sherman*, arriving at Bismarck on Sunday morning, July 31, 1881. Hundreds had gathered to greet the great chief. Yet on this day, Sitting Bull appeared less than noble in the crowd's eyes—and in his own. The Hunkpapa leader wore not his finest clothes of old, for he had none, but instead a dirty white shirt, blue pantaloons, common moccasins, and a set of smoked goggles (to provide some protection for his eyes). To more than a few, Sitting Bull looked freakish.

To others, the chief seemed deflated, defeated. Accordingly, a *Bismarck Tribune* reporter declared, as quoted by Bill Yenne, "Why, he does not look at all like I expected, he don't look as savage as I thought he would. Can that be the instigator of the Custer Massacre?"

From Bismarck, it was on to Fort Yates on the Standing Rock Reservation. Sitting Bull had been assured by the American and Canadian governments that he and his followers would be allowed to remain at Standing Rock, to set up camp there with the rest of the Sioux. For Sitting Bull, it was not to be, however. Instead, the defiant Hunkpapa warrior would not only become a ward of the state, but a prisoner of war.

RESPECTED GUEST

On September 6, Sitting Bull was informed that he and his band of ragged Hunkpapa would not be allowed to stay on the Standing Rock Reservation, but rather they would all be shipped down the river to Fort Randall, to remain there until further notice—as prisoners of the U.S. government. Sitting Bull contemptuously told authorities that he would not go, that he would rather die like Crazy Horse than leave Standing Rock. (Four months after his surrender in 1877, Crazy Horse left the reservation without authorization to take his sick wife to her parents. He was ordered arrested. At first,

Crazy Horse did not resist, but he began to struggle when he real-ized he was being taken to a guardhouse. During the struggle, a sol-dier fatally stabbed Crazy Horse with a bayonet.)

But Colonel Charles C. Gilbert, commander at Fort Yates, took control and on September 9, bayonet-toting infantry bunched Sit-ting Bull and his loyalists together and herded them toward the *Sherman* as it lay docked on the Missouri River. A *New York Times* reporter was on the scene to file the story. "The band was surrounded by a squire of soldiers, and forced, step by step, down the bank and into the boat, which then started down the river to Fort Randall," the correspondent declared. "A nephew of Sitting Bull made some resistance, and was knocked down with the butt end of a musket. A squaw of the band, rendered desperate by the removal, killed her child and tried to commit suicide."

No one in authority could tell Sitting Bull how long he would have to remain at Fort Randall as a prisoner of war. No one knew.

Yet, as humiliating as his stay would be at Fort Randall, Sitting Bull soon found himself being treated more as a respected guest than as a prisoner. The fort's commander, Colonel George Andrews, knew what had really happened at Little Bighorn. The colonel had great respect for the Hunkpapa leader.

While the Lakota were not allowed to hunt at Fort Randall, they were not permitted to go hungry either. Sitting Bull settled down to a routine that let him while away his days having fan mail trans-lated and read to him, now that, for the first time in his life, he had a fixed address to which such letters could be sent. Having learned to write his name, Sitting Bull enjoyed signing autographs for people who wrote to him or made their way up the Missouri River to visit. As Bill Yenne was quick to note, "When the Indians ceased to be objects of fear, they became objects of interest." Sitting Bull had be-come a mysterious and fascinating man, the most famous Ameri-can Indian in the world.

In early May 1883, after 19 months in confinement at Fort Randall, Secretary of War Robert Todd Lincoln (son of the famous president) ordered Sitting Bull released. On May 10, the chief and 171 former prisoners, traveling by steamer, landed at Fort Yates, on

Indian Names

"When Rain-in-the-Face was but a brown-skinned mite, the mother of the mite set him up in the shade of a tree while she got ready the midday meal," James McLaughlin wrote in *My Friend the Indian.* "The mother, engaged in her domestic work, forgot the child for a moment, and a neighbor ran into the tepee to tell her it had rained in the face of her baby. . . . It is a sign, said the child's father. Let him be called Rain-in-the-Face."

In such a manner, Sioux babies acquired their names. Below is a partial list of Sioux Indian signatories to the Fort Laramie Treaty of 1868:

MAH-TO-NON-PAH, Two Bears
AH-KE-CHE-TAH-CHE-KA-DAN, Little Soldier
CH-WI-TO-WIA, Rotten Stomach
SKUN-KA-WE-TKO, Fool Dog
I-A-WI-CA-KA, The One Who Tells the Truth
CHAN-TEE-WE-KTO, Fool Heart
SHUN-KA-KAN-SHA, Red Horse
HI-HA-CAH-GE-NA-SKENE, Mad Elk

the Standing Rock Reservation. They were not exactly free, but they were no longer incarcerated. A wasichu gift house awaited Sitting Bull, his mother, two wives, and many of his children.

FREEDOM'S MANIFESTO

Such a "luxury," if that is what a log house could be called, was of questionable value to Sitting Bull, as well as the many Sioux who had, in previous years, dragged themselves onto reservations, where they were forced to give up their "Indianness" in exchange for bare survival. "By way of curing him of his nomadic habits, he [the American Indian] was given a fixed habitation and coerced into living in a house built by his own hands," James McLaughlin wrote in

The reservation was designed to break the traditional way of life for American Indians, as they could not travel, hunt, or forage outside of their designated area without permission. Sitting Bull was given this house, not a tepee, in Standing Rock Reservation for his family and feared that these restrictions would bring about the end of his people.

his memoir *My Friend the Indian*. "The day the Indian moved out of his airy tepee into the closed-up house in which no provision was made for ventilation of any sort, he reduced his chance of surviving by a considerable percentage."

The reservation system, established in its full manifestation with the Fort Laramie Treaty of 1868, was, with the conclusion of the American Indian wars in the 1880s, all about assimilation, the "civilizing" of indigenous peoples, making them as American as possible. Much of white society, with its "friends of the Indian" associations headquartered in the East, believed it was necessary "to kill the Indian to save the man." Only one standard of civilization existed, that of American whites, and the indigenous peoples must be forced to conform to it.

Central to the assimilation process was the notion of "fixity." The Sioux and other tribes were to remain, as much as possible, immobile. "Indians were not allowed to leave the reservation without a pass from the agent," Louis Warren reported. "Hunting for deer, picking chokecherries, or visiting relatives on another reservation required a personal appeal at Agency headquarters. . . . Along the passage between savagery and civilization, conditions of itinerancy or even migrant labor were trapdoors to barbarism."

These, the white man's restrictions, Sitting Bull had warned about for years. Confinement, he was sure, would result in the eventual destruction of his people. Upon his release from Fort Randall, Sitting Bull issued what, in effect, was a manifesto, extolling the freedom he loved and its nomadic ways, while denigrating the lifeways of the wasichu. As reported in *The Lance and the Shield*, the Hunkpapa declared:

> White men like to dig in the ground for their food. My people prefer to hunt the buffalo as their fathers did. White men like to stay in one place. My people want to move their tepees here and there to the different hunting grounds. The life of white men is slavery. They are prisoners in towns or farms. The life my people want is a life of freedom. I have seen nothing that a white man has, houses or railways or clothing or food, that is as good as the right to move in the open country, and live in our own fashion.

INTERLUDE

"I am going to try hard to get old Sitting Bull," Buffalo Bill Cody told his partner, Nate Salsbury, as reported by Louis Warren. "If we can manage to get him our everlasting fortune is made."

In genuine irony, the freedom Sitting Bull bemoaned the loss of (now that he was bound to a reservation) would become his, if only for a short while, by joining Buffalo Bill's famous Wild West show as it set out on an extensive tour of the East Coast in 1885. The extravaganza, a giant traveling spectacle the likes of which America (and later Europe) had never seen before, featured performances by hundreds of cowboys, vaqueros, and, most important, "real" American Indians. By joining the show, American Indians were quick to understand how it offered a chance to escape reservation travel restrictions, see how the wasichu thought, and earn decent money that could, in turn, be sent back to family members. The Cheyenne and the Sioux (along with other tribes) lined up to join the show. Sitting Bull, now deemed less dangerous and thus able to leave Standing Rock, would join Buffalo Bill for a most successful tour, visiting such cities as New York, Philadelphia, and Washington, D.C.

The chief was paid $50 a week (plus expenses) to tour with the Wild West show, the equivalent of $1,000 in today's money. Most American Indian performers in the show were paid but $25 a month. Yet back home, on the reservation, agency Indian police, who were the highest-salaried American Indians, received only $8 a month. Driving a freight wagon, making butter, or chopping wood paid even less. Sitting Bull's income probably exceeded anything paid to an American Indian at the time.

In addition, the Hunkpapa's contract with the show permitted him to sell autographed photographs of himself at every stop on the multi-city tour. Sitting Bull would often get $5 per picture. Keeping with his tradition of generosity, Sitting Bull frequently gave away much of the money he earned to beggars he encountered. Sitting Bull, coming from a sharing society, could not understand how such prosperous wasichu would have so many poor among them. "The white man knows how to make everything," he told Annie Oakley, the famous female sharpshooter, also traveling with the show, as quoted in *Bury My Heart at Wounded Knee*, "but he does not know how to distribute it."

After the tour, Sitting Bull returned to Standing Rock. With him he took two farewell presents from Buffalo Bill—a large white hat and a performing horse. The horse had been trained to sit down immediately and raise one hoof with the sound of a gunshot.

After moving to Standing Rock Reservation, Sitting Bull (*seated*) was presented with an opportunity to be a part of Buffalo Bill's (*center*) traveling show. As one of the main attractions in this Wild West extravaganza, Sitting Bull earned $50 a week and even more by selling autographed pictures of himself.

In 1887, the most famous American Indian in the world was invited to travel with another Wild West tour, this time to Europe. Sitting Bull declined. He told Buffalo Bull that he was needed at Standing Rock. "There is more talk of taking our lands," he declared, as quoted by Dee Brown.

ALLOTMENT

Sitting Bull had every right to be concerned. By the mid-1880s, 187 reservations existed in the United States, encompassing 181,000 square miles (468,787 square km) and containing 243,000

American Indians. This vast system effectively deprived American Indians of the ability to fight and hunt, to engage in activities that had defined their very way of life.

On the reservations, American Indians lived in mixed, fragmented communities. Their children were forced into agency schools or shipped to boarding institutions in the East, all the better to isolate them from native influences. The American Indians were expected to become herders and farmers. They were encouraged to learn English. Everywhere, American Indians became wards of the state. Many, in response to an unprecedented cultural shock, turned to alcoholism, defeatism, and suicide.

Then, just when it would be hard to imagine that things could get worse, they did. In 1887, Congress passed the Dawes Severalty Act, or the General Allotment Act. Its purpose was simple, and, at first glance, even noble. The act was an attempt to break up the tribes by replacing their traditional communal "ownership" of land for the American system of individual property. Each family would be allotted individual parcels of 160 acres (64 ha), to farm as the *wasichu* did. When every family got their bit of land, what was left over (and it was often considerable) would be given to immigrant settlers. Sitting Bull was right, but it wasn't just "talk" he had heard. Another Indian land grab was in the making.

Allotment was often carried out in bizarre ways. According to Joseph Marshall III, "Once a man signed to accept his 160 acres, he was more or less forced to perform a strange ceremony. He was given a bow and one arrow and taken to a single bottom plow. He was then instructed to shoot the arrow into the distance, throw down the bow, and grab the handles of the plow. The symbolism of casting aside the bow for the plow was obvious. He was casting aside his old identity for a new one. The hunter/warrior was now to be a farmer."

If allotment wasn't bad enough, in 1889 Congress, sensing more was required, authorized the splitting up of the Great Sioux Reservation into six separate reservations (Standing Rock, Cheyenne River, Lower Brule, Crow Creek, Rosebud, and Pine Ridge). Each head of household now got 320 acres (129.5 ha), with the better left-over land being sold to white settlers for $1.25 per acre.

The allotment policy was enforced, in part, by the government's threat to severely reduce rations for their American Indian charges, should they refuse to go along. With reduced rations, and the inability of many American Indian families to turn their acres into subsistent enterprises, by the late 1880s, more than a few reservation Indians were on the verge of starvation.

In response, Sitting Bull, always the defiant one, remained vocal and uncompromising. He argued mightily with American Indian agents whose job it was to force assimilation. Not surprisingly, agents, with one in particular, James McLaughlin, saw Sitting Bull as "crafty, avaricious, mendacious, and ambitious," as quoted in *Indian Wars*. If McLaughlin had a choice, the celebrity Hunkpapa would have been sent off to tour with the Wild West show indefinitely.

HUNKPAPA PATRIOT

James McLaughlin was born in Ontario, became a U.S. citizen, worked as a blacksmith for the U.S. Army, began employment with the Indian Bureau in 1876, and, at the age of 42, arrived to take over as agent at Standing Rock, Sitting Bull's place of residence. The two would maintain a difficult, and at times hostile, relationship to the end.

McLaughlin saw himself as a friend of the Native Peoples, a man chosen to promote, through his guiding hand as an Indian agent, their best interests. Indeed, he titled his autobiography, originally published in 1910, *My Friend the Indian*. Having taken a Dakota wife, McLaughlin was in a particularly advantageous position to present himself as a man who understood the American Indian, his wants, and his needs. He spoke passable Lakota. The Sioux called him White Hair. The short and stocky agent developed a reputation for being strict.

In his autobiography, McLaughlin made it clear how he felt about the American Indian and, in turn, what his purpose and mission was as an agent. "When I entered the service, the military arm was the only power that appealed to the Indian," he wrote. "To the men of my time was appointed the task of taking the raw and bleeding material which made the hostile strength of the Plains Indians, of bringing that material to the mills of the white man, and of transmuting it into a manufactured product that might be absorbed by the nation without interfering with the national digestion. . . . I found that, under the blanket in which the Indian shrouded himself, there was a heart and mind altogether human, but undeveloped."

McLaughlin was clearly a supporter of assimilation. The sooner the indigenous peoples could advance from hunting buffalo, to herding cattle, to growing crops, and, eventually, to developing skills in industry and commerce, the better off not only they, and America, would be.

Not surprisingly, in his dealings with reservation Indians, particularly those he saw as having a leadership position, McLaughlin favored the Sioux who thought as he did, who were willing to concede that the sooner they adapted to the white man's ways, the better. Needless to say, Sitting Bull was not one of McLaughlin favored chiefs. "He professed to be, and was, a thorough hater of the whites," McLaughlin, referring to Sitting Bull, wrote in *My Friend the Indian*. "His medicine was Indian medicine, what the young man wanted, and he got a following altogether out of proportion to his merits as a leader, because he was essentially an unreconstructed Indian."

In McLaughlin's eyes, Sitting Bull remained a hostile, a reactionary opposed to everything McLaughlin believed to be progressive and good for American Indians. The agent was convinced that Sitting Bull was a troublemaker and always would be.

GHOST DANCE

Trouble, as far as the authorities were concerned, came in the form of a new religious movement, one that promised a complete American Indian rebirth.

By the late 1880s, American Indian society was on the verge of collapse. "The reservation had destroyed the very foundations of the Indian way of life," Robert Utley wrote. "The customs, values, and institutions of war and the hunt—overwhelmingly the central concerns of the people in the old days—withered into nostalgic memory. . . . For the loss, the government offered only unsatisfying substitutes: plows, work oxen, log houses, schools, and Christian

After years of forced assimilation on the reservation, it became clear that the old traditional ways of life were quickly fading into memory. Some American Indians, desperate to revive their people's customs, soon turned to a new religion called the Ghost Dance (*shown above*). Led by a shaman who blended American Indian and Christian beliefs, U.S. officials wrongly associated this new religion with an uprising and brutally ended the movement with a massacre at Wounded Knee.

churches, together with an alien, repugnant ideal of what people should strive to be."

Desperate for some sort of salvation, in the winter of 1889–1890, Short Bull and Kicking Bear led a party of 10 Lakota "delegates" off the reservation to Nevada, where they sought out a 34-year-old Paiute shaman known as Wovoka. The shaman, claiming to be the Messiah, offered a dramatic solution, a clear way forward. "All Indians must dance, everywhere keep on dancing," Wovoka declared, as quoted in *Bury My Heart at Wounded Knee*. "Pretty soon in next spring Great Spirit come. He bring back all game of every kind. . . . All dead Indians come back and live again. . . . When Great Spirit comes this way, then all the Indians go to mountains, high up from whites. . . . Then while Indians way up high, big flood comes like water and all white people die, get drowned. . . . Indians who don't dance, who don't believe in this word, will grow little, just about a foot high, and stay that way. Some of them will be turned into wood and be burned in fire."

Thus was born the Ghost Dance religion, a blend of orthodox American Indian belief and the new teachings of Christian missionaries. Short Bull and Kicking Bear brought the Messiah's message back to the Sioux reservations, where it quickly spread. Wovoka had preached peace with the whites, cautioning that in order for the new Promised Land to arrive, one had to live peacefully and non-violently. But, supposedly, others, like Short Bull and Kicking Bear, perverted much of what Wovoka had said, telling followers that they could take on the whites now, without waiting for any flood, and if they wore Ghost Shirts, the garments would make them bulletproof. The authorities, many of whom were quick to believe in the Ghost Dance's supposed hostile intentions, became nervous, fearing a new American Indian uprising.

Sitting Bull neither supported nor denounced the Ghost Dance. McLaughlin, however, seeing a pretext to get rid of his nemesis once and for all, advocated the arrest of the chief. On October 17, 1890, the agent sent a letter to the Commissioner of Indian Affairs. According to Robert Utley, McLaughlin, in paragraph after paragraph, assailed Sitting Bull, calling him "vain, pompous, untruthful, cunning . . . and chief mischief-maker." He urged that, sometime during the winter, Sitting Bull be seized and transported to a military prison far from the Sioux reservation.

BUFFALO BILL RIDES IN

Arresting Sitting Bull would not be easy. If handled badly, it could spark a general Sioux revolt, with violent bloodletting a sure outcome.

Twenty-First Century Reservations

According to 2000 census data, the American Indian population is growing at a quickening rate. As of that census, there were 2,475,956 Native Americans living in the United States. A portion of those individuals are recognized as citizens of 510 American Indian tribes. In turn, 437,079 American Indians live on 314 reservations and trust lands.

A total of 56.2 million acres (22.7 million ha) of land are now held in trust for various American Indian tribes and individuals. The largest reservation is the Navajo reservation, home to 269,202 Navajos. That said, only 10 reservations have a population of 7,000 or more, one of them being the Sioux Rosebud reservation in South Dakota. Most American Indians reside in the western states of California, Arizona, New Mexico, and Washington.

Many reservations, despite gains in health care and education, are straining. According to the Web site *Answers.com*, such reservations "struggled with a fragmented land base because of allotment, a growing hostility from non-Indian residents living on or near reservations, the need for greater economic self-sufficiency, and the task of building stronger cultural identities."

Despite such challenges, many American Indians chose to identify with reservation life because it gave them a strong sense of place. According to *Answers.com*, "There is, across native North America, a new pride in tribal identity and a renaissance of traditions."

With the Ghost Dance in full force, the army had quickly declared martial law on the reservations. It had the primary responsibility to suppress an uprising, should it occur. McLaughlin, however, wanted to handle any arrest of Sitting Bull in his own way, for his own credit, by using his agency Indian Police to do the job. The question, therefore, was who would apprehend Sitting Bull— the Bureau of Indian Affairs or the U.S. Army?

To settle the matter, General Nelson Miles, now commander of the Division of the Missouri, came up with a most creative and, he hoped, effective solution.

On November 28, 1890, Buffalo Bill Cody, fresh from a European tour, showed up with an entourage at Fort Yates. He produced orders, dated November 24 and signed by General Miles, directing him to, as quoted in *The Lance and the Shield,* "secure the person of Sitting Bull and deliver him to the nearest commanding officer of U.S. troops." Cody told officials at Fort Yates that he was to be provided with whatever transportation and protection he requested.

McLaughlin was not happy. Allowing Cody (a high-profile civilian) to receive credit for persuading Sitting Bull to surrender was not something the agent accepted. As a consequence, officers at the fort were "ordered" to provide Cody with plenty of alcohol, all the better to intoxicate him beyond the ability to travel. But Buffalo Bill, it turned out, could hold his liquor better than most, and on November 29 he was off with a wagon-load of gifts to arrest his friend Sitting Bull.

McLaughlin, unbeknown to Buffalo Bill, had launched a backup plan that involved sending telegrams to Washington, in a frantic effort to get Cody's orders rescinded. His efforts were successful. Buffalo Bill had not gone more than five miles (eight km) on his mission when McLaughlin's Indian Police overtook him. The head officer presented a telegram from no less than President Benjamin Harrison, overriding General Miles and recalling Buffalo Bill.

Miles, not at all pleased with the Cody affair, sent a telegram to Fort Yates, dated December 12, directing Colonel William Drum, the commander of the fort, to take responsibility for arresting Sitting Bull. The colonel and McLaughlin devised what they felt was a straightforward plan. The arrest of the Lakota leader would be made by Indian Police, backed by soldiers if needed. December 20, the next ration day, was the date set for taking Sitting Bull into custody.

DEAD AT THE DOOR

Events conspired, however, to push the arrest date up to December 15. At 4:30 A.M., in the cold gray dawn, Lieutenant Bull Head lead 42 "Metal Breasts," as the Indian Police were called, across the Grand River, to the Lakota chief's village, just a stone's throw away from where he had been born 59 years earlier. In a letter to Bull Head, McLaughlin wrote, ominously, as quoted by Robert Utley, "You must not let him escape under any circumstances." A squadron of cavalry waited in reserve a few miles back.

With the police having surrounded Sitting Bull's cabin, Bull Head quickly dismounted, ran to the door, and banged on it with the butt of his pistol. He was let in and found Sitting Bull sitting on the edge of his bed, naked. "Let me put my clothes on and go with you," he told Bull Head, as quoted by Albert Marrin. "I'll go without any resistance." When Sitting Bull reached the open door, however, he hesitated. A huge crowd of noisy, armed supporters had gathered outside.

From inside the cabin, Crow Foot (Sitting Bull's son) stood up. "You have always called yourself a brave chief," he yelled to his father, according to Marrin. "Now you are allowing yourself to be taken by the Metal Breasts."

Sitting Bull hesitated and then forcefully addressed the crowd before him. "I am not going," he declared, as quoted in *Buffalo Bill and Sitting Bull*. "Do with me what you like. I am not going. Come on! Come on! Take action! Let's go!"

Exactly what happened in the next few moments is still open to debate. In the conflict and chaos that ensued, however, Sitting Bull was shot twice. He was felled with a bullet from Bull Head's rifle and, immediately after, from a gun held by Red Tomahawk.

Dead, probably by the time he hit the ground, the last of the defiant Sioux, defender of their cherished way of life, was killed not by vengeful Crow or U.S. soldiers, but by his own people. Upon hearing gunfire, Sitting Bull's gray horse, the trick pony given to him by Buffalo Bill, sat down and raised a hoof.

Convinced that Sitting Bull was stirring up a rebellion by encouraging the Ghost Dance religion, U.S. officials ordered his arrest and capture. Sitting Bull, who neither supported nor opposed the new religious movement, fought his arrest and Indian Police killed him and his son Crow Foot. Red Tomahawk (*left*) and Eagle Man (*right*) both helped kill Sitting Bull during the fight.

A number of Indian Police quickly retreated to Sitting Bull's cabin, where they found Crow Foot hiding under the blankets. The 14-year-old boy begged for his life. Bull Head, mortally wounded in the melee, shouted to his fellow police, "Kill him," as quoted by Bobby Bridger, "they have killed me." Crow Foot, at the age when his father had won his first coup, was dragged from his cabin and shot dead by Indian Police.

In the attempt to arrest Sitting Bull, 12 Hunkpapa, including the chief's adopted brother, Jumping Bull, were killed. So, too, were four Indian Police. Bull Head died of his wounds the following day. "If they had left Cody alone," a soldier, knowing of Sitting Bull's sweet tooth, remarked, as quoted in *Sitting Bull and His World*, "he'd have captured Sitting Bull with an all-day sucker."

HUNKPAPA PATRIOT

It was not yet over. Other arrests had been planned. On December 28, 1890, a detachment of the 7th Cavalry (Custer's old contingent) intercepted Big Foot and a ragged band of approximately 350 cold, tired, and hungry Lakota headed to Pine Ridge to give themselves up. Big Foot, suffering from full-blown pneumonia, was being pulled along on drag poles behind a horse. The Lakota were 15 miles (24 km) from their reservation destination, near a creek known as Wounded Knee.

Armed with four Hotchkiss guns (state-of-the-art, rapid-fire, light artillery capable of firing two-inch, high-explosive shells), the regiment's commander, Colonel James Forsyth, ordered his nearly 500 men to surround the Lakota. When soldiers tried to secure Lakota weaponry by going lodge to lodge in search of guns and knives, tension and anxiety mounted. In the end, fewer than 50 weapons were confiscated.

Exactly what happened next may never be fully known. A shot was fired; some say by a deaf Lakota named Black Coyote who did not know what was going on. In any event, the sound ignited the worst American Indian slaughter since the carnage at Sand Creek in 1864.

In addition to Lakota men, Lakota women and children were fired upon, often at point-blank range. "The outer ring of soldiers began shooting at women and children who had sought shelter in the dry ravine south of the camp at the first sounds of gunfire, and then began to flee as the firing increased," Joseph M. Marshall III reported. "Within scant minutes, an estimated 300 Lakota were killed."

Wounded Knee effectively ended the American Indian's attempt to repel the wasichu, an effort once led by the Sioux's greatest leader, Sitting Bull. All his adult life, the chief sought to retain the old, freedom-loving ways, for him and his people. When James Walsh, the Northwest Mounted Police major who had befriended Sitting Bull in Canada, heard of his death, he wrote an insightful obituary, part of which declared, as reported by Albert Marrin:

> I am glad to hear that Bull is relieved of his miseries even if it took a bullet to do it. A man who wields such power as Bull once did . . . cannot endure abject poverty, slavery, and beggary without suffering great mental pain, and death is a relief. . . . History does not tell us that a greater Indian than Bull ever lived. . . . This man, that so many look upon as a bloodthirsty villain . . . was not a cruel man. He was kind of heart. He was not dishonest. He was truthful. He loved his people and was glad to give his hand in friendship to any man who believed he was not an enemy and was honest with him. . . . The war between the U.S. and Bull was a strange one. A nation against one man. On the U.S. side there were numbers; on Bull's side there was principle.

Jumping Badger, Slow, Sitting Bull—he remained faithful to his culture and to his tribe until the day he died. *Tatanka-Iyotanka*—a true Hunkpapa patriot.

CHRONOLOGY

1831 Jumping Badger is born; as a young man, he is called Slow.

1838 During the "Trail of Tears," 16,000 Cherokee from the southeastern United States are forcibly moved to lands west of the Mississippi River; 4,000 die along the way.

1845 Jumping Badger earns his first coup; he is renamed Sitting Bull.

TIMELINE

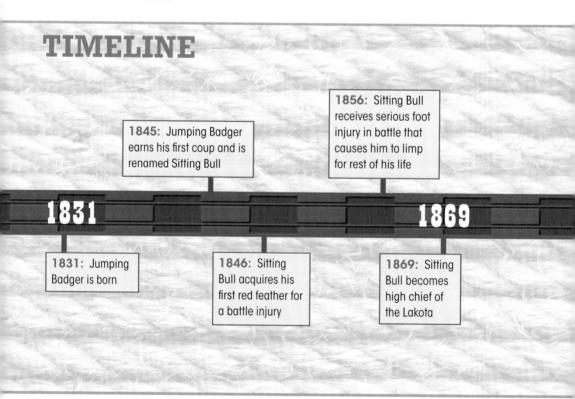

1856: Sitting Bull receives serious foot injury in battle that causes him to limp for rest of his life

1845: Jumping Badger earns his first coup and is renamed Sitting Bull

1831

1869

1831: Jumping Badger is born

1846: Sitting Bull acquires his first red feather for a battle injury

1869: Sitting Bull becomes high chief of the Lakota

1846 Sitting Bull acquires his first red feather for injury sustained in battle.

1851 The Fort Laramie Treaty of 1851, which aims to restrain "hostiles," is signed.

1856 In a battle, Sitting Bull receives a serious foot injury that will cause him to limp for the rest of his life.

1859 Sitting Bull's father dies in battle.

1862 The Santee War in Minnesota inflicts a major defeat on the Sioux, who are driven west.

1864 **July 28** Sitting Bull suffers a defeat in the Battle of Killdeer Mountain.

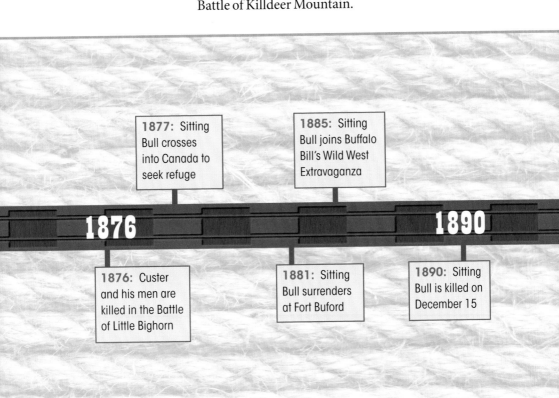

1877: Sitting Bull crosses into Canada to seek refuge

1885: Sitting Bull joins Buffalo Bill's Wild West Extravaganza

1876

1890

1876: Custer and his men are killed in the Battle of Little Bighorn

1881: Sitting Bull surrenders at Fort Buford

1890: Sitting Bull is killed on December 15

November 29   More than 200 Cheyenne Indians are slaughtered in the Sand Creek Massacre in Colorado.

1866   Oglala warriors, led by Crazy Horse, attack and kill 80 U.S. soldiers in the Fetterman Massacre.

1868   The Fort Laramie Treaty of 1868 establishes the Great Sioux Reservation.

1869   Sitting Bull becomes high chief of the Lakota.

1874   Gold is discovered in *Paha Sapa* (Hills That Are Black), also known as the Black Hills, the western third of the Great Sioux Reservation; thousands of miners rush to the region.

1876   **June 25**   George Custer and all 210 of his men are killed in the Battle of Little Bighorn.

1877   **May 6**   Crazy Horse surrenders.

May 7   Sitting Bull crosses into Canada to seek refuge.

Sept 5   Crazy Horse is killed.

1881   **July 19**   Sitting Bull, along with 150 loyal followers, surrenders at Fort Buford.

1885   Sitting Bull joins Buffalo Bill's Wild West Extravaganza.

1887   The Dawes Severalty Act, which distributes land to American Indians in Oklahoma, goes into effect.

1889   The Ghost Dance religious movement begins.

1890   **December 15**   Sitting Bull is killed.

Dec. 29   The Wounded Knee massacre ends American Indian resistance to *wasichu* encroachment.

GLOSSARY

American Indian   The name used to identify the aborigines of North America.

annuity   A sum of money or goods paid on a regular basis.

assimilation   To absorb into a culture or mores of a population or group.

asylum   A place of retreat and security.

badger   A burrowing mammal of the weasel family, mostly found in the Northern Hemisphere.

band   Small-scale societies of hunters and gatherers that generally number less than 100 people.

breechcloth (loincloth)   A cloth worn around the loins in warm climates. In the summer, it was often the only garment an American Indian warrior would wear.

buffalo   Also know as bison; an animal with short horns, heavy forequarters, and a large muscular hump that was abundant on the Great Plains until they were nearly exterminated in the late-nineteenth century. They are now raised commercially.

Buffalo Jump   The herding of buffalo over a cliff some 20 feet (6 meters) or more in height.

clan   A division within a tribe made up of members who are usually related.

coups   A French-Canadian term for signs of victory; they were counted by many American Indian tribes. There were usually three coups: for killing an enemy, for scalping, or for being the first to strike an enemy.

fetish   An object of reverence or obsessive devotion.

lodge   On the American frontier, a rude (unfinished) shelter or abode.

Manifest Destiny   The nineteenth-century belief that it was inevitable the white man should control the American continent from the East Coast to the West Coast.

messiah   A professed or accepted leader of some hope or cause.

moccasin   A soft leather heel-less shoe or boot with the sole brought up the sides of the foot and over the toes.

musket   A heavy large-caliber muzzle-loading firearm, inferior to a rifle.

nemesis   A rival or opponent.

pantaloon   Dlose-fitting trousers worn in the nineteenth century.

pennon   A long streamer typically attached to the head of a lance.

Pincer Movement   A military attack by two coordinated forces that close in on an enemy position from different directions.

piskin   A confined space, such as a corral, where buffalo were herded before slaughter.

quiver   A case for carrying or holding arrows.

scalp   The part of the human head attached with hair; cut or torn from an enemy as a token of victory.

shaman   An American Indian "medicine man," who would use magic to cure the sick, locate the hidden, and control events.

sinew   Known as the tendon, it is the part of a large animal used for sewing, making fish lines, and ropes.

Tatanka Iyotanka   The Lakota name for Sitting Bull.

tepee   A cone-shaped dwelling used by Plains Indians made from skins of animals, usually the bison. (Also spelled "tipi.")

tomahawk   A war-club, an ax, or a club.

tribe   A group of individuals who are bound together in a permanent body, having a unified purpose. A tribe will have a common derivation, customs, and common language.

BIBLIOGRAPHY

Books

Bridger, Bobby. *Buffalo Bill and Sitting Bull: Inventing the Wild West.* Austin: University of Texas Press, 2002.

Brown, Dee. *Bury My Heart at Wounded Knee: An Indian History of the American West.* New York: Henry Holt and Company, 1970.

Deloria, Vine Jr. *Custer Died for Your Sins.* New York: Macmillan Co., 1969.

Gibbon, Guy. *The Sioux: The Dakota and the Lakota Nations.* Malden, Mass.: Blackwell Publishing, 2003.

Gill, Jerry H. *Native American World Views: An Introduction.* Amherst, Mass.: Humanity Books, 2002.

Hassrick, Royal B. *The Sioux: Life and Customs of a Warrior Society.* Norman: University of Oklahoma Press, 1964.

Hoig, Stan. *The Sand Creek Massacre.* Norman: University of Oklahoma Press, 1974.

Johansen, Bruce and Roberto Maestas. *Wasichu: The Continuing Indian Wars.* New York and London: Monthly Review Press, 1979.

Lott, Dale F. *American Bison: A Natural History.* Berkeley: University of California Press, 2002.

Lowie, Robert H. *Indians of the Plains.* Garden City, N.Y.: The Natural History Press, 1963.

Maddra, Sam A. *Hostiles?: The Lakota Ghost Dance and Buffalo Bill's Wild West.* Norman: University of Oklahoma Press, 2006.

Mails, Thomas E. *The Mystic Warriors of the Plains*. Garden City, N.Y.: Doubleday & Company, 1972.

Marrin, Albert. *Sitting Bull and His World*. New York: Dutton Children's Books, 2000.

Marshall, Joseph M. III. *The Day the World Ended at Little Bighorn*. New York: Penguin Books, 2007.

McLaughlin, James. *My Friend the Indian*. New York: Houghton Mifflin Company, 1926.

Neihardt, John G. *Black Elk Speaks: Being the Life Story of a Holy Man of the Oglala Sioux*. New York: Simon & Schuster, 1932.

Ostler, Jeffrey. *The Plains Sioux and U.S. Colonialism from Lewis and Clark to Wounded Knee*. Cambridge, UK: Cambridge University Press, 2004.

Prucha, Francis Paul. *American Indian Policy in Crisis: Christian Reformers and the Indian, 1865–1900*. Norman: University of Oklahoma Press, 1964.

Sandoz, Mari. *These Were the Sioux*. Lincoln, Neb.: University of Nebraska Press, 1961.

Stoutenburgh, John Jr. *Dictionary of the American Indian*. New York: Random House, 1960.

Utley, Robert M. *Custer: Cavalier in Buckskin*. Norman: University of Oklahoma Press, 2001.

———. *The Lance and the Shield: The Life and Times of Sitting Bull*. New York: Ballantine Books, 1993.

———. *The Last Days of the Sioux Nation*. New Haven, Conn., and London: Yale University Press, 1963.

Utley, Robert M., and Wilcomb E. Washburn. *Indian Wars*. New York: Houghton Mifflin Company, 1997.

Vestal, Stanley. *Sitting Bull: Champion of the Sioux*. Norman: University of Oklahoma Press, 1932.

Wallis, William. *Selected Essays*. Sherman Oaks, Calif.: Stone & Scott Publishers, 2004.

Warren, Louis S. *Buffalo Bill's America: William Cody and the Wild West Show*. New York: Random House, 2005.

Weatherford, Jack. *Indian Givers: How the Indians of the Americas Transformed the World*. New York: Fawcett Books, 1988.

Whittaker, Frederick. *A Complete Life of Gen. George A. Custer.* New York: Sheldon & Company, 1876.

Yenne, Bill. *Sitting Bull.* Yardley, Pa.: Westholme Publishing, 2008.

Newspaper Articles

"The Hostile Indian Bands: The Whereabouts of Sitting Bull Still in Doubt." *New York Times*, September 1, 1877.

"The Trouble with the Indians." *New York Times*, September 9, 1877.

"Sitting Bull and His Allies." *New York Times*, January 29, 1878.

"Sitting Bull Not on the War-Path." *New York Times*, January 30, 1878.

"Sitting Bull and His Allies." *New York Times*, February 11, 1878.

"Sitting Bull Nearly Starved." *New York Times*, November 11, 1880.

"Sitting Bull's Waning Power." *New York Times*, January 23, 1881.

"Indians Deserting Sitting Bull." *New York Times*, January 26, 1881.

"Sitting Bull in Canada." *New York Times*, February 13, 1881.

"The Death of Gen. Custer." *New York Times*, May 7, 1881.

"The Death of Sitting Bull." *New York Times*, December 17, 1890.

"Sitting Bull's Deaths." *New York Times*, November 12, 1911.

Films

Sitting Bull. Timeless Media Group, 2008.

Sitting Bull: A Stone at My Feet. Lillimar Pictures, 2008.

Web sites

EyeWitness to History.com: The Battle of the Little Bighorn, 1876. Available online. URL: http://www.eyewitnesstohistory.com/custer.htm

Homeland: Plains Indian Timeline. Available online. URL: http://www.itvs.org/homeland/timeline.html

Homeland: The Lakota Ways. Available online. URL: http://www.itvs.org/homeland/lakota_1.html

Indian Reservation. Available online. URL: http://www.answers.
   com/topic/indian-reservation-2

Mysteries of Canada: Chief Sitting Bull. Available online. URL:
   http://www.mysteriesofcanada.com/Saskatchewan/sitting_
   bull.htm

Native American People/Tribes: The Great Sioux Nation. Available
   online. URL: http://www.snowwowl.com/peoplesioux.html

New Perspectives on the West: Sitting Bull. Available online. URL:
   http://www.pbs.org/weta/thewest/people/s_z/sittingbull.htm

The North-West Mounted Police 1873–1893. Available online.
   URL: http://ns.sgdsb.on.ca/Canadian_History/rcmpforeign
   example.doc

Sitting Bull and the Mounties. Available online. URL: http://www.
   historynet.com/sitting-bull-and-the-mounties.htm

Transcript of Treaty of Fort Laramie (1868). Available online. URL:
   http://www.ourdocuments.gov/doc.php?flash=true&doc=42
   &page=transcript

FURTHER RESOURCES

Keenan, Jerry. *Encyclopedia of American Indian Wars 1492–1890*. New York: Norton & Company, 1999.

Martin, Joel W. *Native American Religion*. New York: Oxford University Press, 1999.

Meadowcroft, Enid Lamonte. *The Story of Crazy Horse*. New York: Grosset & Dunlap, 1954.

Penner, Lucille Recht. *Sitting Bull*. New York: Grosset & Dunlap, 1995.

Remington, Gwen. *The Sioux*. San Diego: Lucent Books, 2000.

Sandoz, Mari. *Crazy Horse: The Strange Man of the Oglalas*. Lincoln: University of Nebraska Press, 1961.

Schleichert, Elizabeth. *Sitting Bull: Sioux Leader*. Berkeley Heights, N.J.: Enslow Publishers, 1997.

Spangenburg, Ray and Diane K. Moser. *The American Indian Experience*. New York: Facts on File, 1997.

Stewart, Mark. *The Indian Removal Act*. Minneapolis, Minn.: Compass Point Books, 2007.

Terry, Michael Bad Hand. *Daily Life in a Plains Indian Village 1868*. New York: Houghton Mifflin, 1999.

Web sites

History by the Minute: Sitting Bull

http://www.histori.ca/minutes/minute.do?id=10174

This Web site shows footage from a film re-enactment of Sitting Bull's life. The film is about a minute long.

Plains Indian Web Site

http://www.saskschools.ca/~gregory/firstnations/tipi.html
This Web site gives a detailed description on how a Plains Indian tepee was set up, what was in it, and how the tepee was moved.

Sitting Bull and the Mounties

http://www.historynet.com/sitting-bull-and-the-mounties.htm
This Web site gives a detailed, extensive description of Sitting Bull and his relationship to the Canadian Mounties of western Canada.

PICTURE CREDITS

Page

9: Interfoto/Alamy

13: Mary Evans Picture Library/Alamy

17: Werner Forman/Art Resource, NY

24: Butler Institute of American Art, Youngstown, OH/The Bridgeman Art Library

27: Woolaroc Museum, Oklahoma, USA/Peter Newark Western Americana/The Bridgeman Art Library

31: Peter Newark American Pictures/The Bridgeman Art Library

38: Peter Newark American Pictures/The Bridgeman Art Library

42: Peter Newark American Pictures/The Bridgeman Art Library

47: Peter Newark American Pictures/The Bridgeman Art Library

50: © Library of Congress Prints & Photographs Division, [LC-DIG-ppmsc-02522]

56: Getty Images

59: Bettmann/CORBIS

63: Bettmann/CORBIS

68: Niday Picture Library/Alamy

74: Getty Images

76: © Library of Congress Prints & Photographs Division, [LC-USZCN4-37]

80: Look and Learn/The Bridgeman Art Library

86: Denver Public Library, Western History Collection, D.F. Barry, B-142

92: Denver Public Library, Western History Collection, D.F. Barry, B-142

95: Denver Public Library, Western History Collection, D.F. Barry, B-142

100: Corbis

105: Denver Public Library, Western History Collection, D.F. Barry, B-142

INDEX

A

allotment policy, 96–97
American Horse, 48–49, 70
Andrews, George, 90
animals as models, 14
arrows, 13
assimilation, 92–93, 99
Assiniboine, 34, 82

B

Battle of Fort Rice, 44–45
Battle of Killdeer Mountain, 39–40
Battle of Little Bighorn, 65–68, 88
Battle of Slim Buttes, 70
Battle of the Hundred Slain, 48
Battle of the Rosebud, 60–62
Battle of Wood Lake, 38
Benteen, Frederick, 66, 67
Big Foot, 106
bison. *See* buffalo
Black Coyote, 106
Black Hills *(Paha Sapa),* 55–57, 69
Black Kettle, 41, 62
Black Moccasin, 76
Black Moon, 60

Black Shield, 76
Blackfeet, 51
bows and arrows, 13, 40
Bozeman, John M., 46
bravery, 18–19
buffalo (American bison)
  decline and demise of, 64, 84–85
  fighting qualities of, 18
  scared away by *wasichu,* 71
  uses of, 12, 52
buffalo hunting
  with bow and arrow, 13
  horses and, 12–13
  by Slow, 15
  by sportsmen, 64, 84–85
  traits of best hunters, 14
"buffalo runners," 12–13
Bull Head, 104–106

C

Canada. *See* Grandmother's Country (Canada)
Chase-by-Bears, 18
Cherokee, 26–28

Cheyenne
  in Battle of Little Bighorn, 67
  Fetterman Massacre, 48
  horse expertise, 21
  massacre by Mackenzie, 75
  Prairie Dog Creek conference, 76–77
  Sand Creek Massacre, 41–43
  at Sioux confederation council, 51
Chivington, John, 41, 43
circle of life, 16
Civil War, 37
Cody, Buffalo Bill, 84–85, 93–94, 103
Colorado Territory, 41
compassion, 34
counting coup, 7–8, 32
coup, counting, 7–8, 32
courting, 36–37
Crazy Horse
  in Battle of Little Bighorn, 65, 67
  in Battle of the Rosebud, 61
  in Canada, 58

Cheyenne refugees and, 75
death of, 89–90
girls and, 36
as "hostile," 47–49, 51
as second in command, 53
surrender of, 77
Crook, George ("Three Stars Crook"), 60–61, 69, 74–75
Crow, 7–8, 33–34, 34–35, 61
Crow Foot, 87, 104–106
Custer, George Armstrong, 55, 61–68, 88
"Custer Avengers," 69
Custer Hill, 67

D

Dakota Sioux, 10, 38
Dawes Severalty Act (1887), 96–97
De Smet, Pierre-Jean ("Black Robe"), 49
decoy tactics, 48
Department of the Interior, U.S., 43
Drum, William, 103
Dull Knife, 75

E

emotional distress, 21
etiquette, 24
Evans, John, 41

F

Fetterman, William J., 48
Fetterman Massacre, 48
Finerty, John F., 61
fixity, 93

food, sharing of, 22
Forsyth, James, 106
Fort Abraham Lincoln, 55
Fort Berthold, 44
Fort Buford, 46–47, 87
Fort C.F. Smith, 46
Fort Ellis, 54
Fort Fetterman, 74–75
Fort Laramie, 46
Fort Laramie Treaty (1851), 30–33
Fort Laramie Treaty (1868), 51, 55, 91, 92
Fort Phil Kearny, 46
Fort Randall, 89–91
Fort Reno, 46
Fort Rice, 44–45, 51
Fort Stevenson, 46–47
Fort Yates, 89, 90–91, 103
fortitude, 19–21
Four Horns, 51–52
friendship, 22

G

"Galvanized Yankees," 44
Gaul, 67
General Allotment Act (1887), 96–97
generosity, 22–23
Gets-the-Best-Of, 54
Ghost Dance religion, 99–101, 102
Gibbon, John ("The One Who Limps"), 60–61
Gilbert, Charles C., 90
gold rush, 39, 46, 55
Grandmother's Country (Canada)
arrival in, 77

buffalo decline in, 84–85
forays into United States from, 85–87
Sitting Bull's surrender, 87
Walsh as Mountie in, 79–83
whiskey traders and Mounties in, 78–79
Greasy Grass (Little Bighorn), 65–68
Great Council, 69
Great Indian Treaty Council at Fort Laramie, 30–33
Great Sioux Reservation, 51, 57, 96–97

H

hanblecheya ("crying out for a vision"), 20
Harrison, Benjamin, 103
He Dog, 36
Her-Holy-Door, 8
Hohe (Stays Back, later Jumping Bull), 34, 35, 60, 106
honesty, 22
horses, 11–12, 14, 15, 21
Hundred Slain, Battle of, 48
Hunkpapa tribe
Battle of Killdeer Mountain, 39–40
in Battle of Little Bighorn, 66–67
De Smet as emissary to, 49
divisions within, 44
Fort Laramie Treaty and, 32

horses and, 12
within Lakota, 11
prisoners at Fort
  Randall, 89–91
Strong Hearts
  Society, 33–34
warriors in, 7–8
hunting. *See* buffalo
  hunting

I

Indian Bureau, 43–44
injuries in battle, 33–34
itancan-in-chief
  position, 51–53

J

Jumping Badger (Sitting
  Bull), 8
Jumping Bull (father),
  34–35
Jumping Bull (Hohe,
  adopted brother), 34,
  35, 60, 106

K

Kicking Bear, 100, 101
Killdeer Mountain,
  Battle of, 39–40

L

Lakota Sioux, 10–11,
  32, 44
Lakota Way, the
  bravery and counting
    coups, 18–19
  fortitude and the
    vision quest, 19–21
  generosity, 22–23
  spirituality, 16–18
  wisdom, 23–25
Lame Deer, 76
Lame White Man, 67
land ownership, 96–97

Last Stand Hill, 67
Light Hair (Pretty
  Door), 36–37
Lincoln, Robert Todd,
  90–91
Little Bighorn, Battle of,
  65–68, 88

M

Macdonald, John, 78
Mackenzie, Ranald S.
  ("Three Fingers"), 75
Manifest Destiny,
  29–30, 43
Many Horse, 37
McLaughlin, James
  ("White Hair"), 97,
  98–99, 101–103
Metal Breasts (Indian
  Police), 104–106
Mexican-American
  War, 29
Miles, Nelson ("Bear
  Coat"), 73–74, 103
Mills, Anson, 70
Miniconjous, 48, 51, 73,
  76–77
"mooning," 48
Mounties (Northwest
  Mounted Police),
  78–79

N

Nakota Sioux, 10, 38
names, Indian, 24, 91
Newcomb, Tom, 22
nomadic life, 11, 93
Northwest Territories,
  Canada, 78–79

O

Oakley, Annie, 94
Oglala Lakota, 47, 51,
  67, 76–77

Oregon Trail, 28–29
Otis, Elwell S., 71

P

parleys, 70–71, 73
Pawnees, 30, 75
peace talkers
  (*wolakotiye
  woglakapi*), 30
Peno Valley, 48
"permanent Indian
  frontier," 26, 28, 29
Pinto Horse Butte, 80
Police, Indian,
  104–106
polygamy, 37
Power River country,
  46–48, 69
Prairie Dog Creek,
  76–77
property, 22, 96–97

R

railroads, 53–54
Red Bear, 76
Red Cloud, 47–49, 55,
  77
Red Cloud's War,
  47–48
Red Tomahawk, 104
Reno, Marcus, 66–67
reservation system,
  49–51, 92–93, 95–97,
  102
Rosebud Valley, 58,
  60–62

S

San Arc Sioux, 51, 73,
  76–77, 81
Sand Creek Massacre,
  40–43
Santa Fe Trail, 29
Scott, Winfield, 26

Seventh Cavalry, 64–68, 106

Sheridan, Philip, 62

Shirt Wearers council, 51–52

Short Bull, 100, 101

Shoshone, 61

Sibley, Henry Hastings, 38

silence, 8–10

Sioux Nation, 10–11, 32

Sitting Bull *(Tantanka-Iyotanka)*
  arrest of, 101–104
  birth of, 8
  childhood of, 7–8, 14–15
  death of, 104, 107
  elected itancan-in-chief, 51–53
  marriages, 36–37
  Miles's description of, 73–74
  names for, 7, 8
  surrender of, 87, 88–89

Slim Buttes, Battle of, 70

"Slow" (nickname), 7, 14

"smoking party," 53–54

Snow on Her, 37

spirituality and religion, 14, 99–101

Spotted Eagle, 54, 76, 81

Standing Rock Reservation, 89, 90–91, 94–95, 98

Strong Hearts Society, 33–34

Sully, Alfred, 39, 44

Sun Dance, 17–18, 20, 58–60

sweat lodge ceremony, 72

Swift Cloud, 34

T

tepees (tipis), 83

Terry, Alfred ("One Star Terry"), 60–61, 62–63, 69

Trail of Tears *(Nunna dual Tsuny),* 26–28

V

Vestal, Stanley, 18, 37, 44, 49, 53

virtues, cardinal (Lakota)
  overview, 18
  bravery, 18–19
  fortitude, 19–21
  generosity, 22–23
  wisdom, 23–25

vision quest, 20, 72

W

Wagon Train of 1843, 29

Wakan Tanka (Great Spirit), 14, 16–18, 58, 60

Walks Looking, 37

Walsh, James M. ("White Forehead"), 79–83, 85–87, 107

war chief, Sitting Bull made, 34

War Department, U.S., 44

warfare, Sioux, 32. *See also specific battles*

Washburn, Wilcomb, 30

Washita River, 62

wasichu (white man), encroachment of, 24, 39, 69. *See also specific battles*

westward expansion, 28–30, 43–44

whiskey traders, 78–79

White Bull, 54, 58, 71, 73, 76

White Dog, 82–83

Whitman, Marcus, 29

Wichasha Wakan (holy man), 20

Wild West Show, Buffalo Bill's, 94–95

wisdom, 23–25

wives of Sitting Bull, 36–37

Wood Lake, Battle of, 38

Wooden Leg, 58

Wounded Knee massacre, 106–107

Wovoka, 100–101

Y

Yanktonnais Sioux, 85

Yellowstone River region, 53–54, 64, 71

Young Man Afraid of His Horses, 49

ABOUT THE AUTHOR

Ronald A. Reis has written young adult biographies of Eugenie Clark, Jonas Salk, Lou Gehrig, Mickey Mantle, and Ted Williams, as well as books on the Dust Bowl, the Empire State Building, the New York City Subway system, African Americans and the Civil War, and the World Trade Organization, all for Chelsea House. He is the technology department chair at Los Angeles Valley College.